THE ULTIMATE LONG-DISTANCE DADS GUIDE

How to Build Strong Bonds — Whether You're Divorced, Living Apart, or Always on the Road

Drs. Danny R. Andreas Msc.

Parantas
Making distance parenting work

Praise For The Ultimate Long-Distance Dads Guide

The Ultimate Long-Distance Dads Guide provides a hands-on toolkit for fathers who want to actively build and maintain a close bond with their children, even across physical distance. It's written for divorced dads as well as for fathers who are frequently away from home — for example, due to work commitments. It may also be useful for separated mothers seeking a new perspective, or for professionals working with separated families.

Right from the start, the author – Drs. Danny R. Andreas, MSc. – makes one thing clear: fatherly presence does not end with physical separation. Strong emotional bonds are still possible. The book is currently available in English and deliberately avoids legal paragraphs. A German edition is in preparation.

What stood out most to us are the 25 actionable strategies. These range from meaningful video-call rituals to age-appropriate gift ideas and peaceful child handovers.

A clear thread throughout the book is respect for the mother. This aligns with our experience in family support: negative remarks not only damage the co-parenting dynamic but also put the father-child relationship at risk. Naturally, this is something both parents and their respective circles need to uphold.

Sensitive topics such as parental alienation and gatekeeping are openly addressed and supported with de-escalating, practical solutions — a big plus, since these are common challenges in our daily advisory work.

Another positive aspect: the author clearly favors mediation over long, drawn-out court battles. He emphasizes shared parental responsibility as a central theme. This shifts the focus back to the parents' duty — and the child's right — to have a meaningful relationship with both parents. That is a core concern of Väteraufbruch für Kinder e.V.

Conclusion: The Ultimate Long-Distance Dads Guide is a motivating and practical compass for dads who live far from their children – and maybe even for moms.We welcome this book because it supports the implementation of cooperative parenting, especially after separation or divorce.

Christoph Köpernick, Board Member of Väteraufbruch für Kinder e.V., vaeteraufbruch. de

Danny Andreas' The Ultimate Long-Distance Dads Guide is a wonderful resource for fathers who are "distanced." This could be fathers who travel for work or separated fathers who are in close proximity but are being alienated from their children. The same principles apply in having to work to create and maintain a meaningful bond with your children.

His advice, informed by his own experience, is thoughtful and creative at the same time simple and practical. He relays what I have told 100s of fathers – you need to work your short, intermediate and long-term goals at the same time.

For those fathers who find themselves in protracted battles to be more actively involved in their children's lives, this book can help you make the most of the limited contact you have with your children.

Jeff Steiner, Executive Director Dads' Resource Center, dadsrc.org

Cover design by: Danny Andreas

Photography Portrait Author and Portrait Dr. Judit Gaál

by Rajna Tamás

Published by Parantas

Amsterdam, The Netherlands

ISBN: 979-8-8996-5998-0

For information, permissions, or bulk orders, contact:
info@parantas.com

*To my dearest one in the world,
my greatest reason,
my truest joy,
and the heartbeat behind every
word in this book.*

Preface

In the quiet corners of our lives, where miles stretch between a father's heart and his child's, a unique story unfolds. This book, "The Ultimate Distance Dad's Guide," is born from a deep understanding of that story — a journey I've witnessed firsthand with its author, my esteemed former client. Our shared history spans years, a long road we've travelled together, even facing the unprecedented challenges of the COVID-19 pandemic.

I remember his little girl taking her first unsteady steps; now, she has blossomed into a young woman. Through legal battles and emotional tides — including the isolating times of the pandemic — we faced a shared struggle. It's a testament to the enduring bond between parent and child, even when distance and global events cast their shadows.

If you find yourself in this space, feeling the ache of separation due to work's demands or the complexities of divorce, know this: you are not alone. This book is a beacon, a hand reaching out across the miles to offer solace, understanding, and a path forward. More than just emotional support, it offers real-world strategies to stay present, maintain strong communication, and nurture your bond — no matter how far apart you are.

Inside, you'll find practical steps you can take to create meaningful moments and build a resilient relationship with your child. Within these pages, you'll discover insights and strategies, not just to cope, but to actively cultivate connection and turn the sour lemons of circumstance into the sweet refreshment of lemonade. This is for every father who carries his child in his heart, no matter the distance or the challenges life throws their way. Wishing you an insightful read, as advocate and fellow traveller on this journey,

— Dr. Judit Gaál, Family Law Attorney

Contents

Distance Fathering Challenges 79

Today's Landscape of Long-Distance Fathering 105

The Future of Remote Fathering   115

Preparing for Evolving Parenting Dynamics 123

Introduction

Welcome

Hi Dad,
I'm really glad you made it here. Just by opening this book, you've already shown that you take your role as a father seriously — whether you're divorced, separated by distance, or working far from home.

That alone says a lot. It means you're ready to go the extra mile for your child. And that matters more than you might realize. By the end of this book you will understand that it makes all the difference.

My name is Danny Andreas. I'm a 55-year-old devoted long-distance father, and the founder of Parantas and Distancedads.com. Despite the many challenges distance brings, I've managed to build and maintain a close bond with my 10-year-old daughter — even though we live more than a thousand kilometers apart (about 620 miles).

It hasn't been easy. Our journey as a long-distance father and child has had its ups and downs. But every effort has paid off. My daughter grew up bilingual, embraced my native culture, and when she first visited my home country, she felt at home straight away. That deep connection has always been our anchor.

It's also what motivated me to dive deep into how to be the best dad I could be from a distance. Over time, I developed practical strategies that actually work.

Things like creative time management, consistent virtual visitation routines, and using communication technology to bridge the physical gap.

As the years went by, I noticed more and more fathers — from all over the world — facing the same struggles. Many were searching for support after divorce, or trying to understand parental alienation, legal complications, and how to handle the emotional weight of guilt and loss.

Groups started forming — Facebook pages, forums, networks — where dads could connect, share, and look for answers. Some focused on rights and advocacy. Others offered emotional support or practical guidance. And being an expat dad myself, I saw how distance and cultural differences made things even harder. Divorce rates among international couples are higher, and cross-border custody laws add extra layers of stress.

Writing has always helped me process things, so I started a blog — Distancedads.com. I began sharing what I'd learned: personal stories, useful tools, and insights I picked up along the way. Within a few months, thousands of fathers from over 50 countries had visited the site. The blog grew and then expanded with videos, podcasts, and social media channels — reaching more than a million streams.

The overwhelming response made one thing obvious: Fathers are forever. Our role doesn't end with distance or divorce — it evolves. That's why this book came together — to bring all those lessons into one place, easy to access, and made just for you.

English isn't my first language, but reaching as many dads as possible has always been my goal.
To make my writing as accessible as I can, I've used a mix of translation and editing software.
I've also avoided complex words when simpler alternatives work better.

What to Expect

I'm not a counselor, therapist, or lawyer. But I do bring real-world experience and a deep passion for learning. I've always been a researcher at heart — testing what works, questioning what doesn't, and turning theory into action. That's what this book is built on.

It's not a step-by-step manual because every father's journey is different. But what it does offer is a set of guiding principles, clear strategies, and practical tools that you can shape to fit your own Fathering Journey.

Throughout the book, you'll find insights drawn from my experience — backed by research and shaped by real-life practice — along with links to helpful resources and deeper reading at the end of each section and again at the end of the book, if you want to explore further.

What You Will Learn

By the end of this book, you'll have a better understanding of:

- How to prepare for the unique challenges of distance fathering

- Why your role as a father still matters deeply — no matter the miles

- Simple, effective ways to stay connected to your child

- How to deal with legal and custody obstacles

- What to do if you're facing parental alienation

- Managing your mental wellbeing and emotions

- The realities of distance fathering in today's world

- How tech, such as AI and communication tools can help bridge the gap

- How to find dad support and dad-centered resources

- Practical strategies that make long-distance fathering more effectivein

I hope this book brings you some clarity, inspiration, and peace of mind. Above all, I hope it reminds you that your love matters — and your presence, even from afar, makes all the difference.

Let's get started.

How to Prepare to Be a Distance Dad?

Where to start?

So, you're facing the reality of being a distance dad. You might wonder how best to get ready for this journey.

Since every situation is different, there isn't one simple answer. However, I've found that the best preparation starts with understanding the playing field you're stepping into.

Learning about common experiences and best practices from other dads helps a lot. By reading this book, you've already taken a great first step.

In order to understand the situation which you are in, let's have a look at why dads become distance dads and what the landscape looks like.

Why do dads become distance dads?

There are usually two main reasons:

Divorce

Many fathers find themselves living apart from their children after a divorce or separation. Often, one parent moves away, increasing the distance.

Given that an average of 50 percent of marriages end in divorce, and mothers often get primary custody, this path is common. These non-custodial dads usually get a visitation arrangement.

Work Obligations

Work obligations are the second major reason. Jobs in the military, trucking, entertainment or off shore often require long periods away.

Expats, corporate executives, pilots, and traveling salespeople also face this. These dads are often still married but spend extended time away from home.

This book is for any dad living apart from his child, married or not. Long-distance marriages often face added pressure, which can lead to separation or divorce, especially those involving foreign cultures or intercultural relationships.

The Big Picture

It helps to understand the broader picture too. Statistics show many children live apart from their fathers. In the UK, it's about 1 in 5 kids. In the US, it's roughly 1 in 6.

Respect for children

Globally, up to 25% of children grow up without their biological fathers nearby. By 2030, it's estimated that 580 million children will lack father figures in their daily lives.

As distance fathering becomes more common, it's concerning, especially given the growing body of research on how crucial fathers are to their children's development.

Besides an average divorce rate of 50 percent and the fact that 40 percent of children are born outside of the marriage, there are several additional factors which influence who becomes a distance dad.

- Age can play a role. Younger dads might focus on education or careers that lead them away. Older dads might have jobs requiring frequent travel.

- Education and income levels also matter. Pursuing degrees or specific careers can mean relocating.

- Cultural norms are important too. Some cultures accept fathers working abroad, leaving families behind temporarily or permanently.

- Societal changes like globalization also impact families.Increased mobility means parents and kids might live apart for work or study. These trends bring opportunities but also require adaptation from both fathers and children.

Preparing means acknowledging these realities. It involves understanding why you are in your situation and learning from others who have walked this path. It requires recognizing the global societal trends and your individual personal factors at play. Most importantly, it involves committing to being the best dad you can be, despite the distance.

This book will guide you through the specific challenges, which you will or might face and offer practical strategies to deal with them.

———————

Key Findings:

- Preparing to be a distance dad involves self-education and understanding the landscape.

- Key factors include the primary reasons for separation — such as divorce or work.

- Demographic elements like age, education, and culture also play a role.

- Societal shifts, especially increased mobility, contribute to the trend.

- Recognizing these aspects helps you anticipate challenges and build effective strategies.

———————

Why Are Dads Important?

When I first became a distance dad, I really questioned my role. How could I be important from far away? I knew fathers played a critical part in their children's lives.

We offer unique contributions that shape who they become. But living apart adds extra challenges. It takes effort to fulfill that essential role across the miles.

In this section, we'll explore ten key reasons why dads matter. We'll also look at how we, as distance dads, can still make that vital impact.

1 - Setting the standard for future relationships

We dads often set the standard for future relationships. The way you interact with your child shapes their expectations.
How to treat the other parent also matters, even after separation. Positive interactions build trust and healthy patterns.

Tip!

From a distance, focus on quality time during calls and visits. Make sure to show respect for others, especially the mom. Keeping promises is vital. It shows reliability and builds a foundation for trust. Regular, thoughtful communication helps reinforce these standards.

2 - First Male Role Model for Daughters

For daughters, dads are often the first male role model. A loving father shows his daughter what respectful relationships look like.

He helps her build self-worth and expect kindness from men.

Tip!

Ensure regular, meaningful contact. Share stories highlighting positive male behavior. Talk about what respect and integrity mean in relationships and/or about different perspectives between men and women.

3 - Help Sons Shape Character

For sons, fathers are key in shaping character. Boys often look to their dads to learn how to be men.

A father's presence helps build discipline, strength, and resilience. This fosters confidence and self-worth and guides sons toward responsibility. Living apart means I must be intentional during our time together.

Tip!

Keep your word, always. Whether you engage in challenging projects or sports, even online. Encouraging his interests shows you care and support his growth.

4 - Encouraging Self Reliance

Dads often encourage independence and confidence. We tend to push exploration a bit more than moms might.

Involved fathers help children build self-sufficiency. This prepares them for life's challenges.

Tip!

Even from afar you can set small challenges for your child between visits. During calls you can celebrate successes. Make sure your child knows you're here for guidance when needed. This helps build your child's confidence step-by-step.

5 - Provide Stability and Security

Our role in emotional development is huge. We provide rules, security, and a sense of pride.

Supportive dads positively impact cognitive and social growth.

We teach long-term emotional resilience and problem-solving. Maintaining this connection requires extra effort from a distance.

Tip!

Schedule regular private chats with your child. Talk about their best and worst moments, exploring the feelings involved. Make sure to connect before and after big events. Tell your child that it can discuss anything with you.

6 - Teach Discipline and Responsibility

Discipline and responsibility are other areas where dads contribute uniquely. We often enforce rules and teach about consequences.

This helps develop accountability and a strong moral compass.

Enforcing rules from afar requires teamwork. Clear communication with the other parent is essential.

Tip!

During our visits and online chats, we discuss risks and consequences. We agree on rules and the consequences for consistency. I use video calls to reinforce accountability, while encouraging goal-setting and rewarding effort to teach responsibility.

7 - Encouraging Physical and Intellectual Challenges

Fathers often encourage physical and intellectual challenges.

We tend to engage in more stimulating, rough-and-tumble play.

This type of interaction teaches problem-solving and resilience. It helps kids push their limits and build confidence.

Distance makes physical play tricky, but not impossible.

Tip!

Plan active things for your visits. Between visits, create intellectual challenges during online meetings or hire an online language teacher. Encourage your child to try new sports, hobbies or activities.

8 - Providing a Sense of Security

Providing a sense of security is fundamental. Dads contribute to both physical and emotional safety.

This stability allows children to explore the world confidently.

We offer a sense of protection and strength. From afar, consistent contact is key. Keeping every scheduled call or visit is crucial.

Tip!

Frequently reassure your child of your love and support. Being involved in your child's daily life, even virtually, builds that security. Communicating with the mom ensures a stable environment.

9 - Role Model for Work Ethic

We are also important role models for work ethic and perseverance.

Kids learn by watching our dedication and resilience. They see how we handle challenges and keep going.

Mothers often model multitasking, while fathers might exemplify focus and determination.

Tip!

Share your own challenges and successes. Talk about your work and how you handle difficulties. Encourage your child to set goals and praise their efforts, reinforcing these values.

10 - Create lifelong Memories and Traditions

Finally, dads create lifelong memories and traditions.

Shared hobbies, family rituals, and spontaneous simple moments strengthen our bonds.

These experiences shape identity and provide a sense of belonging.

While moms often create stable routines, dads might introduce unique adventures. Distance requires creativity here.

Tip!
Make your online time high-quality and interactive. Plan memorable activities for your visits. Create shared projects you can work on remotely. Taking lots of photos and videos builds a library of tangible memories.

Key Findings:

- We are fundamentally important to our child's development.

- We influence their future relationships, character, and confidence.

- We provide emotional support, discipline, and a sense of security.

- We encourage challenges and model perseverance.

- We create lasting memories.

- We can fulfill these vital roles, even as distance dads.

Final Thoughts on How to Prepare to Be a Distance Dad

Being a distance dad isn't something most of us planned. It's a path we find ourselves on — often unexpectedly — after a divorce, a job move, or life taking a different turn. But here you are, showing up anyway. That says everything.

You've taken the time to understand the reasons, the realities, and the impact that comes with distance fatherhood.

That insight alone already puts you ahead. It shows you're not just going through the motions. You want to show up in a way that matters — and that commitment will be your greatest strength.

The truth is, distance doesn't define your fatherhood.

What defines it is your effort. Your consistency. Your willingness to learn, adapt, and keep showing up. That's what your child will remember — the calls, the honesty, the laughter you shared across the miles.

In the chapters ahead, we'll dig into practical ways to build and protect your bond, even when life pulls you apart physically.

You'll find strategies that work, not just for surviving this journey, but for turning it into something meaningful.

You're not alone on this road. Millions of dads are walking it too. And while no one can do it for you, you'll have support, tools, and stories to lean on as you go.

You've already taken the first step. For further reading on the topics in this section, check out the **Sources and References** at the end of this book.

How to Be a Distance Dad?

How to make long distance fathering work?

How do you actually do this? How do you parent effectively when miles separate you from your child?

When I first faced this situation, I felt lost. My child lived over 1,000 miles away, and I had no prior parenting experience. I wondered how I could build a strong relationship under these circumstances.

Many resources describe long-distance parenting, but few address the specific challenges we dads face. These are often quite different from those faced by mums. I researched extensively, used my common sense, and got creative. Over the past ten years, I developed strategies that worked well for my child, the mum, and me.

25 proven strategies

These 25 strategies helped me build and keep a meaningful bond with my child. Using them will save you time, effort and money and give you and your child peace of mind.

Even though everyone's situation is unique, these are basic and generic guidelines, which will only benefit your cause and never harm you. My hope is they will support you in becoming the best distance father you aspire to be. Let's dive in.

Treat it like an important job commitment. You cannot afford to be late or miss meetings.

Failing to follow the plan disappoints your child. Avoid trying to change things frequently. This can backfire, potentially giving a non-cooperative mother grounds to object. It could even harm your standing in court proceedings.

Tip!

Set multiple phone calendar reminders before each meeting. This trains your brain to anticipate contact time.

3 - Communicate with the Mum

Maintain regular communication with your child's mother, if possible. Never use your child as a messenger between parents. This puts your child in a harmful loyalty conflict and exposes them to adult issues.

You don't need to be best friends to communicate effectively. Think about colleagues you communicate with professionally. A friendly relationship is a huge plus for the child, allowing open discussion.

Tip!

Even if the relationship is strained, keep communication lines open. Restrict talks to essential topics if needed. Your child's well-being and safety depend on it.

4 - Use Email for Communication

Email is often the best channel for communicating with the mother. It gives you time to think before responding. Reread your drafts before sending them. Words written in anger can cause damage.

1 - Create a Parenting Plan

Distance creates unique hurdles for us divorced distance fathers. A detailed long-distance parenting agreement is a powerful tool.

It helps maintain a strong connection with your child. It also helps avoid conflicts with your child's mother.

Think of it as an agreement outlining your (contact) rights and (financial) obligations as the non-custodial dad.

Visitation Arrangement

A Parenting Plan usually includes a visitation arrangement or a co-parenting schedule, which offer stability.

Creating a Parenting Plan and visitation schedule brings clarity and peace of mind for everyone involved.

Family Care Plan

Good practice is to include a family care plan, which lists all the important people who are part of the child's care team including the parents, family and friends, and the child's health care providers.

Tip!

Make sure your plan includes flexible cancellation terms. Life happens — illness, travel issues, or unexpected changes. Flexibility means you and your child can easily reschedule missed visits or calls. A clear plan saves stress and avoids disappointment.

2 - Follow the Parenting Agreement

Once you have a parenting agreement, consistency is crucial for your child. Stick to the visitation schedule diligently.

Ask yourself if you still feel so strongly after cooling down. This helps keep communication factual and avoids emotional battles.

Tip!

In high-conflict situations, avoid phone calls or brief text messages. Email creates a written record of your communication — something that can serve as legal proof in court if disputes arise later.

5 - Tone Your Voice Down

If communication is difficult, adopt a business-like tone. This helps avoid emotional triggers.

Try to avoid lengthy arguments altogether. Email can act as a discussion blocker, especially with a formal approach.

Tip!

Use "I" statements to express your feelings or thoughts. For example, "I feel concerned when..." instead of "You always...". Avoid accusatory "you" statements. I found using a simple, polite email template helped manage my own anger and frustration.

6 - Neutralize Transitions

Sometimes, pick-ups and drop-offs at the mother's home cause conflict.

The physical presence of both parents can create tension. If this happens repeatedly, consider alternatives.

Tip!

Arrange transitions at a neutral location, like a library or park. Another option is having a neutral third person handle the handover. Avoiding stress for your child is truly worth the effort.

7 - Manage Conflicts

When conflict erupts, step back if possible. Schedule a discussion for a calmer time.

Trying to reason with someone during high emotion rarely works.

Remember, you might not be the true cause of the conflict. You might have just triggered an underlying issue.

If you cannot resolve things, consider mediation or other dispute Alternative Dispute Resolution (ADR) methods. This can save lengthy and costly court battles.

Tip!

Sometimes, the best action is inaction. Saying and doing nothing can prevent escalation.

8 - Be Consistent with Mum's Rules

Support the mother's decisions in front of your child. This provides consistency and stability, even if you disagree. This can be very tough. Especially with differing views on parenting, religion, or culture.

But presenting a united front is vital for your child. It prevents them from playing one parent against the other.

Tip!

This doesn't mean you can't have your own house rules during visits. Explain to your child that some rules differ, just like at school. Children adapt to different rules in different settings.

9 - Do Not Be Negative About Mum

Avoid speaking negatively about the mother in your child's presence. It is incredibly harmful to them, because they are half the child of their mother.

If this is hard, simply don't discuss her with your child. If your child brings her up, respond neutrally or positively. Be mindful; children are sensitive and sense insincerity.

10 - Support Your Child

Children are naturally curious. This offers many bonding opportunities for a father.

Young children need to explore the world. You get the privilege of introducing new things and experiences.

Think of yourself as a guide on a safari. Show your child exciting places during meetings.

Teach your child to have self-worth by praising it for accomplishments how little they may be.

Tip!

Support whatever your child wants to investigate. Children often develop intense but short-lived obsessions. Roll with it and show enthusiasm for their current passion.

11 - Schedule Video Calls

Regularly schedule video calls. This maintains strong communication with your child and gives both of you something to look forward to.

Tip!

Use technology creatively during video calls. Create personalized 'shows' or play educational games together. Make the calls engaging and interactive, not just passive viewing. (Look for ideas on 'Video Call Parenting'.)

12 - Be Adventurous

Make each physical visit an adventure. Explore different playgrounds, zoos, museums, or parks.

Create memorable moments and experiences. Give your child exciting "first times," like their first plane ride or concert or horse riding.

Tip!

Plan visit activities together with your child beforehand. Offer options and let them choose. Use pictures or videos to build excitement.

13 - Be in the Moment

Every time together is precious. During visits or video calls, give your child your full attention. Put away distractions.

Show genuine interest in what your child says. Listen actively and ask follow-up questions.

This provides reassurance and validation. Offer plenty of hugs and verbal expressions of love. This builds emotional safety.

Tip!

During our calls, I often ask my child about the best thing that happened that day. Friends are always a great icebreaker — kids love talking about them. These stories can reveal what your child values in others, or which traits they might still be figuring out in themselves.

14 - Send Surprises

Surprise your child with thoughtful gestures. Send cards or small gift boxes occasionally. Unexpected surprises often mean more than holiday gifts.

They don't need to be expensive.

A simple "thinking of you" gift shows you care. Remember preferences change quickly. Ask them before buying expensive items.

Tip!

Check returned items sections online or browse second-hand stores for budget-friendly finds.

15 - Get Creative

Consider crafting gifts instead of always buying them. This allows you to create something personal.

It can be tailored specifically to your child's interests.

Making something by hand feels fulfilling. It infuses the gift with Dad love, making it more meaningful.

Tip!

If scissors and glue aren't your thing, try editing music or videos for your child — like I did. Or print some of your favorite images to share with them.

16 - Learn How to Present a Gift

Pay attention to gift presentations. For children, the unwrapping experience is a big part of the joy.

Try to use nice packaging.

Wrapping paper doesn't need to cost much. It significantly enhances the overall experience.

Tip!

If wrapping isn't your strength, pick a store where they wrap it nicely for you. Or enlist a friend to help you make it look special.

17 - Let Them Decide

Instead of always choosing a gift yourself, try this. Surprise your child with a trip to a store.

Let them pick their own gift within a set budget. This can also apply to experiences. Let them choose a restaurant or activity.

Since my child could talk, I've offered choices. This ensures we both enjoy our time together.

Tip!

Your priority is quality time and your child's happiness. Offer a few options you both like and let your child choose. This also helps you manage your budget effectively.

18 - Stay Involved

You can stay involved in your child's life from afar. Keep track of school progress, activities, and important events.

Ask about their friends, teachers, and neighbors. Knowing the key people in their life shows you care.

Tip!

Learn the names of your child's favorite teachers. Asking about them specifically opens doors. You can learn a lot about your child's daily school life this way.

19 - Foster Social Connections

Help your child keep connected with close relatives, such as grandparents and establish new connections in your location (if applicable).

Or help maintain connections in their location. Get to know their friends' parents if possible. This can help arrange playdates during visits.

When visiting my child abroad, I had no local network initially. I frequented playgrounds daily. Gradually, I met another distance dad with a child the same age. Over the years, we built friendships and now celebrate birthdays together. I also started an online facebook group for local parents with bilingual children. This connected me with another distance dad friend. Be proactive in finding or creating a community.

20 - Respect Their Privacy

Respect your child's privacy, especially as they grow older. Avoid pushing for information they aren't comfortable sharing.

This is tough for distance dads hungry for details. I've seen my own child enter the pre puberty years. The shift in attitude and need for privacy is real.

What about online activity? I treat it like letting my child go to the park alone.

I've managed to safeguard my child's internet privacy and app usage, with parenting control apps.

Also I have educated my child about the risks involved when using the internet.

Tip!

Educate your child about online security. Before granting full privacy, ensure they have skills to protect themselves. Build their resilience. And put a piece of black tape on the cam of their devices!

21 - Sit on Your Money

Being a distance father often involves significant expenses.

Travel costs, especially flights, add up. Strict budgeting and smart planning are essential to guarantee visits.

Look for cheap tickets well in advance.

Consider airline loyalty programs for perks like lounge access. This saves money on airport food and drinks.

Some airline credit cards let you earn miles and pay over time.

Tip!

Don't buy gifts last minute, especially at airports. Start looking for deals right after your last visit. Keep an eye out for discounts throughout the year. This removes pressure and saves money.

22 - Be Realistic About Your Role

Acknowledge the inherent challenges of distance fathering. Be kind to yourself; you're likely doing your best.

You will spend less time with your child than most resident dads. That's a fact.

Your role is often complementary to the mother's role. Support your child in ways that add to their primary care. Don't underestimate the importance of this support.

Remember, quality time matters more than quantity.

Some married dads work long hours and see their kids less than you might.

Tip!

If you are fully present during calls and visits, you provide immense quality. Leverage that focused time to build a strong bond.

23 - Be Flexible in Your Approach

Flexibility is key for a distance father. Visits are planned far ahead, but unexpected things happen.

The COVID pandemic was a massive challenge for us all. How do you connect when travel and touch are restricted?

During that time, my child and I increased video calls. I sent weekly gift boxes. Those were extreme circumstances, hopefully rare.

Tip!

Develop a mindset that's ready for the unexpected. Be flexible and think of solutions when things shift. I always keep a plan B in my back pocket.

24 - Be Patient

Patience goes hand-in-hand with flexibility. Allow your child time to transition at the start and end of visits.

Be patient with the mother.

Don't push excessively if she's slow providing information. Sometimes, withholding information can be used negatively. Especially if you seem desperate for it.

Tip!

In my experience, asking less often yields more information eventually.
25 - Enjoy Solo Time

One potential upside of distance fathering is having free time. Use the time when your child is with their mother for yourself. Pursue hobbies, travel, relax, and recharge.

You are not a 24/7 hands-on parent. You don't have to act like one constantly. I think about my child often throughout the day, lovingly.

I trust they are well cared for by their mum. I don't worry excessively.

Tip!

Allow yourself time to de-stress and shift your focus sometimes. A rested, fulfilled dad is a better dad during connection times.

Final Thoughts about How to Be a Long Distance Father

Being a distance father definitely presents real challenges.

We deal with setting up schedules, communicating across miles, and fostering connection despite separation. But it's absolutely possible to build and maintain a strong, loving bond. It requires the right approach and a positive mindset. By using the 25 strategies, you can manage the complexities with more confidence.

Creating a solid parenting plan, communicating effectively, managing conflict constructively – each step matters. Patience, flexibility, and a commitment to adapting are crucial. Always prioritize your child's well-being. Maintain consistency in your interactions. This creates a nurturing environment that distance cannot break.

While it has challenges, distance fathering also offers chances for unique connections and shared experiences. Embrace these opportunities. Stay committed to your relationship with your child. You can make this journey successful and create lasting, positive memories together. I truly hope these insights help you on your own fathering path.

For further reading on the topics in this section, check out the **Sources and References** at the end of this book.

How to Keep Connected

Effective Remote Communication Techniques

When you're a distance dad, staying emotionally close to your child takes extra effort. You can't rely on casual daily moments.

Every interaction needs to carry more meaning.

Over time, I've found that there's no one-size-fits-all solution.

What works for a toddler may not work for a teenager.

And what feels natural to you might not always match your child's needs at that stage in their life.

Whether it's through video calls, sending a thoughtful gift, or sharing something physical like a favorite puppet or t-shirt with your face on it—there are many ways to stay connected.

The tools might be digital or analog. Some take planning, others are spontaneous.

But the key is understanding how to connect in ways that match your child's age, attention span, and emotional needs.

This section covers the full range—from fun call setups to creative gift-giving—tailored to what makes sense developmentally.

Communication with children

I learned quickly that I needed creative ways to make the calls with my then seven months old child fun and meaningful.

Over the years, I've discovered several techniques that truly work using various tools. These methods helped me build a strong bond with my child despite the miles. Here are some proven tips I hope will help you too.

Turning video calls into personal broadcasts

One major breakthrough for me was turning video calls into personal broadcasts. Young children get bored watching a static talking head. They need varied sensory input.

I found free software like OBS (Open Broadcast System) incredibly helpful.

It lets you set up different scenes with videos, pictures, or screen captures. Think of it like creating a mini-TV show just for your child.

You can add simple frames or interactive elements. Your face can still be visible in a corner, so your child sees you. Tools like VoiceMeeter Banana help improve sound quality.

Using video call platforms like Microsoft Teams, Google Meet, or Zoom alongside OBS is great for making the actual calls. Many of these platforms also have themed backgrounds possibilities and allow recording.

It might seem technical initially, but online tutorials make it manageable. The goal is to make the call as playful and as visually stimulating as possible.

Reading stories remotely is different from having your child on your lap. They can't point at pictures or turn pages easily.

Simple storytelling needs visuals to work well online. You can find free children's e-books online and make slideshows for OBS or use screensharing in Teams, Meet, Zoom.

Interactive Family Apps

Beyond standard video calls, family apps like Caribu or Kinzoo offer built-in games and activities in a child-safe environment.

They come with a wide range of content, but the downside is that you're limited to what the app publishers provide. Unlike tools like OBS, you can't share your own personal videos or content which you really care about.

Using AI for storytelling

Using AI tools, such as ChatGPT, Gemini, Co-pilot or OpenArt.ai to generate custom fairytales is amazing. You can base the story on your child's favorite words or recent experiences.

Children love hearing and seeing their own ideas woven into a narrative or slideshow. This really captures their attention.

This technique even works well for regular phone calls without video. I found making stories interactively with my child and AI was key.

Hand puppets are fantastic tools for connecting with toddlers. They live in a magical world where toys come alive. Puppets can communicate ideas or introduce concepts in a fun way.

You don't need fancy puppets; an old sock with eyes works fine. Give the puppet a name, maybe let your child choose it.

Combining Analog and Digital Communication

I once printed photos of my facial expressions onto a teddy bear's t-shirt.

I sent the bear to my child. During calls, my child showed me the bear.

It helped us connect my face on the screen with a physical object.

Investing in a few puppets to reenact familiar stories also works wonders.

It takes preparation but makes calls much more interactive.

Never underestimate the power of music.

Children respond to music and rhythm long before they master language. Singing favorite songs provides comfort, joy, and familiarity.

Pay attention to your child's reactions. You'll quickly learn their preferred tunes.

Don't be surprised if they ask for the same song repeatedly. Repetition is crucial for learning at that age.

Playing music they love makes the call a positive experience. It strengthens your emotional connection across the distance.

Singing songs is also a great way to introduce them to your native language if this is different from the mother tongue.

Sharing your personal world

As a distance dad, you miss out on many shared real-life experiences. But you can create virtual ones.

Children love animals. If you can't visit a zoo together, visit one yourself.

Film the animals, talk about them, maybe even show yourself feeding them.

Share this personal video during your call. Your child will enjoy this virtual tour guided by you.

You can do this with anything interesting: your house, workplace, or town.

Become your child's personal, private influencer, sharing your world with them.

Celebrating Birthdays & Holidays

Celebrating birthdays and holidays remotely can feel challenging. But you can make these occasions special.

Upload a background theme to Teams, Meet or Zoom or use software like OBS to show virtual decorations, such as balloon frames or animations to your video feed.

Create a pretend cake with real candles. Let your child blow them out 'through' the screen.

Find themed content or use real props. Dress up in hats, wigs, or costumes.

Using humor through props is a great way to connect. It helps bridge the distance and create fun, shared memories.

Key Findings:

- Effective remote communication goes beyond simple conversation.

- Turn video calls into engaging mini-broadcasts using free software like Teams, Meet, Zoom in combination with OBS.

- Explore specialized family apps like Caribu or Kinzoo that integrate activities.

- Make storytelling interactive with AI-generated tales or hand puppets.

- Use music and singing to connect emotionally and teach languages.

- Create personal vlogs for your child, such as trips to the zoo or your job.

- Celebrate special occasions creatively with virtual decorations and real props.

- These techniques require effort but make remote interactions fun, meaningful, and relationship-building.

The Perfect Long Distance Gifts: How Science Can Help You

Choosing gifts for your child from far away feels like a constant puzzle.

For us distance dads, a gift isn't just an object. It's a means of communication with our children.

It's a way to say "I love you," "I'm thinking of you," "I care about you," across the miles.

But because we miss daily interactions, knowing what message will resonate can be tough.

This is especially true with infants, toddlers, who have not clearly established preferences yet.

How can we ensure our gifts communicate our connection effectively?

Using science and understanding in which stage of development your child is offers valuable clues. Let's look at how to choose gifts that send the right message for each age.

Infants and Toddlers (0-24 Months)

Communicating Comfort and Connection

At this age, children are rapidly developing senses and basic bonds. Gifts should communicate safety, comfort, and engagement with their world.

When my child was this young, choices felt broad. They can't tell you preferences yet.

Offering variety helps you learn what connects.

Gift Criteria as Messages

- Sensory toys (textured books, musical items) communicate "I want to engage with your world."

- Soft toys or blankets holding your scent strongly communicate "I am close, even when away," offering comfort.

- Simple learning toys (shapes, colours) communicate "Let's explore together."

- Easy-to-ship gifts or items you bring on visits communicate "This is a special time with Dad."

Toddlers to Preschoolers (2-4 Years)

Communicating Shared Fun and Learning

Language booms now, alongside imagination and early social play. Gifts can communicate support for their expanding world. My child was pure energy at age two!

A Scuttlebug ride-on toy communicated "I see your energy, let's have fun!" It was foldable, perfect for visits – communicating adaptability too.

Gift Criteria as Messages

- Language-focused toys (books, puzzles) communicate "I support your learning to talk and think."

- Imaginative toys (blocks, costumes) communicate "Let's create worlds together."

- Interactive learning apps or toys communicate "We can learn and play together, even apart."

- Active toys (balls, ride-ons) communicate "Let's enjoy playing more actively."

Early Childhood (5-7 Years)

Communicating Understanding and Shared Interests

Thinking becomes more complex; reading and problem-solving emerge. Interests can change rapidly! My child jumped from Paw Patrol to Marvel fast. Keeping up was a challenge. Gifts need to communicate "I pay attention to what you love right now."

While giving merchandise I noticed, I also sought gifts communicating intellectual challenge with a science, technology, engineering and mathematics (STEM) focus. A tablet was huge. It communicated "Let's stay connected," and crucially, "I support you learning anything in my language," as my child watched Dutch, my native language, content on it.

Gift Criteria as Messages

- Educational games communicate "Learning can be fun, let's challenge ourselves."

- Creative kits (art, crafts) communicate "I value your creativity, show me what you make."

- Simple STEM toys communicate "Let's explore how things work," perhaps together on visits.

- Interactive books communicate "I support your growing mind."

Middle Childhood (8-13 Years)

Communicating Respect for Individuality

A stronger sense of self, hobbies, and independence develop.

Gifts should communicate respect for their evolving identity.

I saw my child change clearly here. One day dolls, the next pre-teen interests! Asking their opinion on gifts communicates "I respect your views."

Giving a budget communicates "I trust your choices." Gifts chosen by them communicate ultimate validation.

Gift Criteria as Messages

* Advanced STEM toys communicate "I support your complex interests."

* Hobby-related gifts (sports gear, art supplies) communicate "I see your passion, keep going."

* Deeper books or kits communicate "Let's explore subjects you like."

* Tech gadgets for shared play communicate "Let's connect through shared activities."

Adolescence (14 Years & Up)

Communicating Trust and Shared Experiences

Identity formation, complex relationships, and future thoughts dominate.

Gifts should communicate trust, recognition of their maturity, and a desire for connection.

My child is almost a teen, but with nieces and nephews, I know pleasing them is tricky. Knowing them well is vital.

If unsure, money or gift cards communicate trust.

Offering to shop together communicates "I want to share this experience with you," making it more personal.

Gift Criteria as Messages

- Skill-focused gifts (coding lessons, advanced kits, courses) communicate "I support your future growth."

- Personalized items communicate "I see your unique identity."

- Gifts offering shared experiences (tickets, travel) communicate "I value our time together."

- Financial gifts with guidance communicate practical support and trust.

Making Your Message Clear (and Saving Money)

Giving gifts effectively also means being practical.

These tips help ensure your message of love isn't lost, while being budget-conscious.

- Shop Year-Round: Gives you time to find thoughtful gifts without pressure — and stay within your budget.

- Consider Refurbished/Secondhand: Saves money while still offering quality and value.

- Invest in Wrapping: A low-cost way to build excitement and make the gift feel extra special.

- Smaller, Creative Gifts: Stretch a small budget further. Every gift becomes a memorable experience.

- Involve Your Child: Makes the gift more meaningful and saves money by avoiding unwanted items.

- Give a Budget: Encourages independence and decision-making — and can be a fun activity if you do it together.

- Observe and Listen: Kids often mention what they truly enjoy or need — just pay attention.

Key Findings:

- Long-distance gifts are effective tools for communication with children.

- Understanding your child's developmental stage helps tailor the message.

- Gifts convey emotions like comfort, shared fun, learning support, respect for individuality, trust, and a desire for shared experiences.

- Thoughtful gift selection ensures the message of love and connection is clear.

- Smart shopping strategies ensure the message is delivered effectively and sustainably.

Engaging in Your Child's Education and Activities

Staying involved in your child's education and activities from afar isn't easy. You're not there for school runs, football games, or daily homework.

But being a distance dad doesn't mean being absent. It means showing up in creative, meaningful ways—even when you're miles apart.

Start with the basics

Celebrate your child's school report, no matter what the grades say. Praise their effort, not just results. You can ask questions about their classes, what they enjoy, and where they're struggling. Show that you care about their learning journey.

Technology can be your best ally

Offer help with homework through video calls. You might even tutor them in a subject you know well.

A short weekly study session keeps you connected—and shows you're invested in their growth.

Many kids love showing off their knowledge to someone who's genuinely interested. That someone can be you.

When you visit, join in

Bring them to school in the morning or pick them up in the afternoon, during visits. These simple moments mean a lot to your child.

It proves that you are for real and not a mythical invisible person. Join a parent–teacher meeting if it falls during your stay. Or arrange a video call with their teacher to stay in the loop.

Extracurricular activities matter too

Attend their soccer game, dance show, or school play if timing allows. If not, ask for photos or videos. React. Cheer them on.

Let them consistently know you're proud. That's how you build a strong emotional bond.

Create Memories

And don't forget—your visits can be full of firsts. Try new experiences together. Ride a horse. Visit a zoo. Go ice skating. Let your child help plan the adventure. Give them options.

Make a little itinerary with pictures or videos so they can get excited.

It builds anticipation and makes the time feel special. And don't forget to record these experiences.

Being in the moment matters

When you're with your child, turn off distractions. Focus on them.

Listen. Laugh. Ask questions. Show you're there, not just physically but address their emotional needs too.

Tip!

Before each visit, plan a small schedule together. Give your child choices. Use photos, maps, or video previews. It makes everything more fun and personal.

Key Findings:

- Distance doesn't mean disconnection. Small actions build big bonds.

- Celebrate school progress—focus on effort, not just grades.

- Help with homework during calls—show you care about their learning.

- Join events when you can, and cheer from afar when you can't.

- Plan visits together—give choices, build excitement, create memories.\

- Be present—listen, laugh, and connect without distractions.

———————

Making the Most of Physical Visits

When you finally get to see your child in person, it's a big moment.

You've probably counted down the days. Your child has too—even if they don't always show it.

These visits aren't about doing something grand.

They're about being fully present and enjoying meaningful time together.

Reconnecting with children

Reconnecting with your child after being apart for a while can be challenging, but it's also a precious opportunity to rebuild your relationship.

From my experience, the key is to keep your expectations low and approach the situation with patience.

It's important to show your child that you're relaxed and not forcing them into anything they're not comfortable with yet.

Just because they don't immediately jump into play or give you affection, it doesn't mean they won't later.

Children, especially babies and toddlers, have short-term memories, and their development happens quickly. What seems like a cold response at the moment could turn into warmth and engagement just a little while later.

One of the ways to ease the transition is to create tangible memories of your time together.

For younger children, visual records like photos and videos are invaluable. Showing your child these moments later can help them relive the experience and associate it with positive feelings.

I remember when my child was a toddler, and we hadn't seen each other in months. I'd sit in the living room and read one of her favorite books aloud. Before long, she'd crawl into my lap, and we'd read together.

We'd slowly build up from there—playing, going for a walk, or visiting my apartment.

As she grew older, she began to understand what to expect from our visits, and I was always amazed at how quickly she adjusted. There was never any anxiety about transitions; it became something we both looked forward to.

Tip!

Take It Slow and Be Present - Reconnecting takes time. Don't rush it. Keep your expectations in check, and let your child dictate the pace. Every small interaction, even if it seems insignificant at first, builds trust and love. Be patient, and focus on being present rather than achieving grand moments.

Emotional Needs

A simple trick is leaving something with a familiar scent, like a worn shirt or a hat. Babies and toddlers are particularly sensitive to smells, and this can help them feel more connected to you when you're not around.

Quality vs Quantity

I've learned that quality matters more than quantity. One afternoon where you're truly there—no distractions—can mean more than a whole week of being half-present.

When my child was very young, I used to plan every visit down to the minute: activities, meals, bedtime routines. At that age, they needed predictability. So did I.

Later, when we got into the flow, I could sometimes let go of the schedule. Those unplanned moments turned out to be the best ones.

At first, I aimed for a new playground every day. But later I saw how simple, spontaneous moments—like sitting on a bench eating ice cream and chatting about nothing—became the most memorable.

Give Options, Not Orders

Let your child make small choices. Instead of buying a gift ahead of time, take them to a toy store or a park and let them decide.

The same for activities. That little freedom brings joy and shows you what matters to them.

It doesn't always have to cost money. A walk, a bike ride, baking cookies, or watching a movie with popcorn—these things create lasting memories. What truly matters is how you make them feel: safe, seen, and loved.

One of the most important things I've learned is to be in the moment. Put away your phone. Don't check email or social media.

Don't multitask. You won't get that time back—and they'll notice when you're not really with them. Show up with your full attention, and you'll give them a memory that lasts.

Friends of Children

Learning the names of your child's friends and getting to know their parents can provide several benefits. It allows you to understand more about your child's developmental stage and behavior, and it also ensures you'll have a better chance of arranging playdates.

Showing interest in your child's social circle not only helps you stay involved in their world, but it also strengthens the bond between you.

However, it can become tricky if the parents of your child's friends are close with your ex-spouse.

This situation can sometimes create challenges, but it's important to remember that acting with sincere respect and good intentions usually leads to positive outcomes in the end. Most parents want what's best for their children. If you approach the situation kindly, they're likely to appreciate your efforts.

Tip!

Consider organizing a birthday party for your child each year—ideally, even if it's a little late. Invite your child's closest friends and their parents. Over time, this gesture can help you build lasting positive relationships. In my experience, these small efforts go a long way in fostering goodwill and acceptance.

Key Findings:

- Physical visits are golden. Make them count, not crowded.

- Reconnection takes time. Don't rush it, just be open and patient.

- Emotional presence beats a packed agenda.

- Let your child choose what you do together. It builds trust.

- Unplug fully. Your attention matters more than any activity.

- Little moments can become big memories.

Final Thoughts about How to Keep Connected

Being a distance dad is challenging, but staying connected doesn't have to be. Over the years, I've discovered that meaningful connections come from creativity and consistency. Whether it's through turning video calls into engaging mini-broadcasts, choosing gifts that communicate love and presence, or actively participating in your child's education and activities, every effort counts.

Using tools like OBS for dynamic video calls has allowed me to create memorable interactions with my child.

Incorporating AI storytelling, hand puppets, and music kept our time together fun and stimulating. These moments became cherished memories that strengthened our bond despite the miles.

Selecting the right gifts also played a crucial role. Understanding my child's developmental stage helped me choose presents that communicated comfort, support, and shared experiences. From sensory toys when they were an infant to tech gadgets as they grew older, each gift carried a message of love and connection. Staying involved in my child's education and extracurricular activities further reinforced our relationship.

Celebrating their achievements, helping with homework via video calls, and attending events whenever possible showed them that I cared deeply about their growth and happiness.Making the most of physical visits was equally important.

Quality mattered more than quantity; being fully present during our time together created lasting memories. Simple, spontaneous moments often turned out to be the most meaningful.In reflection, the key takeaway is that emotional closeness transcends geographical boundaries.

By leveraging technology, thoughtful gifting, active involvement, and quality time, we can build strong, enduring relationships with our children.

For further reading on the topics in this section, check out the **Sources and References** at the end of this book.

How to Tackle Legal Hurdles and Custody

Understanding Custody Arrangements

Being a dad at a distance comes with its own legal maze. Custody papers, support payments, visitation terms—they all sound cold and official. But behind those words are real-life decisions about how often you get to see your child, how involved you can be, and how supported your child feels.

I've learned that the more I understood the legal setup, the less powerless I felt. It didn't solve everything, but it helped me hold my ground.

I could ask better questions, push for fairer terms, and build a setup that made sense for both of us.

This section breaks it down in plain language.

We'll look at what custody actually means, how child support works, and how to set up a visitation plan that fits your situation—not just the court's checklist.

The goal isn't to turn you into a lawyer. It's to give you enough clarity to stay present in your child's life—emotionally and legally.

Physical vs. Legal Custody

There are generally two types of custody: physical and legal.

Physical custody refers to where your child lives.

Legal custody involves decision-making power regarding their education, health, and general welfare.

In my experience, it's important to understand both because they directly impact your role as a dad.

For instance, having joint legal custody ensures you remain involved in critical decisions, even if you live far away.

Courts typically prioritize the child's best interests when determining custody arrangements, in a divorce settlement. Factors like parental involvement, living conditions, and your ability to co-parent often come into play.

From personal experience, sharing a video compilation of my visits with my child in court helped show my ongoing commitment to being present.

Changing Custody Arrangements

Negotiating custody doesn't always have to be adversarial. Mediation, for example, allows both parents to work together with a neutral third party to create a plan that works for everyone.

This approach is the most cost effective and least damaging in the long run. Though for mediation it's impertinent that both parties want to come to legal agreements.

In 2024 I interviewed Dr. Judit Gaál, a family lawyer with more than 35 years experience in divorce settlement and divorce mediation

She explains the difference between a Law Suit and Divorce Mediation as follows:

"Dr. Gaál: A family court lawsuit can last several years. This, while a divorce mediation procedure can be completed in a few months. A shorter procedure usually means substantial lower fees. Moreover, the impact on the parties' future lives differs significantly; a court battle often leads to ongoing conflict, while a mediator provides divorce support and encourages cooperation."

Ultimately, custody isn't just about legal agreements; it's a framework for maintaining a meaningful relationship with your child.

By focusing on cooperation and prioritizing your child's needs, you can build an arrangement that supports long-term connection despite the distance.

Key Findings:

- Custody includes physical (where the child lives) and legal (decision-making authority).

- Courts focus on the child's best interests in a divorce settlement, considering factors like parental involvement and stability.

- Mediation can help avoid conflict and high legal fees by fostering collaboration between parents.

- Consistent effort strengthens your case and reinforces your bond with your child.

Child Support: 10 Things Each Dad Should Know

Child support is one of the most critical yet misunderstood aspects of parenting after divorce.

Over the years, I've learned that being informed can make all the difference in ensuring fairness for both you and your child.

While it may seem overwhelming at first, understanding the basics can help you approach this responsibility with confidence.

Child support isn't just about money—it's about providing stability and meeting your child's needs. Whether you're paying or receiving it, the goal is always to prioritize their well-being.

Here are ten key things every dad should know about child support.

1- Know how child support is calculated

Each state or country has its own formula, often based on income, custody arrangements, and the child's needs.

Research your local laws or consult a lawyer to understand what applies to your situation. Often municipalities or states provide online calculation tools.

2 - Keep detailed financial records

Track all payments, receipts, and expenses related to your child. This documentation can protect you in case of disputes or misunderstandings down the line.

3 - Communicate openly with the other parent

Clear communication about finances helps reduce conflict.

If possible, agree on major expenses like education or medical costs outside formal child support agreements, making them easier to manage and oversee.

4 - Understand modifications are possible

Life changes—job loss, medical emergencies, or shifts in custody—can warrant adjustments to child support orders.

Don't hesitate to seek legal advice if your circumstances change.

5 - Prioritize consistency over perfection

Even small, regular contributions matter more than occasional large payments. Consistency builds trust and shows commitment to your child's future.

6 - Be aware of tax implications

Child support payments typically aren't tax-deductible for the payer or taxable as income for the recipient.

Understanding this can help you plan better financially.

7 - Avoid using child support as leverage

It's easy to let emotions cloud judgment, but tying child support to visitation or personal grievances harms your relationship with your child and their other parent.

8 - Use technology to simplify payments

Tools like direct deposit, apps, or court-ordered systems ensure timely, transparent transactions and proper documentation, minimizing stress for everyone involved.

9 - Stay involved beyond the check

Money is important, but emotional presence matters just as much. Attend events, stay connected virtually, and show interest in your child's life.

10 - Seek professional guidance when needed

If you're unsure about any aspect of child support, consult a family law attorney or mediator.

Key Findings:

- Child support ensures your child's needs are met, fostering stability and security.

- Understanding calculations, maintaining records, and staying consistent are essential practices.

- Open communication and avoiding emotional entanglements lead to smoother co-parenting relationships.

- Professional guidance can clarify complex situations and prevent future conflicts

Visitation Rights and Crafting Effective Schedules

Unlike a Family Care Plan, Visitation rights are often one of the most emotionally charged aspects of a divorce settlement.

Over the years, I've learned that having a clear, well-thought-out visitation agreement is crucial for maintaining consistency and reducing conflict.

It's not just about securing time with your child—it's about creating meaningful moments that strengthen your bond.

Knowing your rights

The first step is understanding your legal visitation rights. These rights vary depending on your local laws, but they generally outline how often and under what conditions you can see your child.

In my experience, being proactive in negotiating these terms early on helped me establish a stable routine.

For example, agreeing on holidays, school breaks, and regular weekend visits ensured I stayed connected with my child without unnecessary disputes.

Crafting an effective schedule requires flexibility and communication. While it's tempting to aim for perfection, life often gets in the way.

Quality over Quantity

My advice? Focus on quality over quantity. A few well-planned visits can be more impactful than frequent but rushed interactions.

Try to coordinate with the child's mum to align your schedules around key events like birthdays, school performances, and family milestones.

Shared Calenders

Technology also plays a role here.

Shared calendars or apps designed for co-parenting make it easier to track visitation dates, adjust plans, and avoid misunderstandings.

This approach keeps everyone on the same page and minimizes stress for both you and your child.

Ultimately, visitation isn't just about seeing your child—it's about making every moment count.

By prioritizing their needs, you ensure that your time together, whether physical or virtual visitation, remains valuable and fulfilling.

Common Schedule Types

Sole Custody Arrangements

Typical patterns:

- Every other weekend (Friday PM to Sunday PM)

- One weekday evening (dinner + homework help)

- Split summer vacations (e.g., 4-6 week blocks)

Shared Custody Options

Popular 50/50 rotations:

- 2-2-3: 2 days with Parent A, 2 with Parent B, then 3 with Parent A (repeats)

- Week-on/Week-off: Simpler for school-age children

- 3-4-4-3: Balances longer and shorter stretches

Long-Distance Considerations

When parenting across 1,000+ miles, there are additional challenges. Here's how I handled some of them:

- Cluster visits (e.g., monthly weekends +2 days, split holidays)

- Always include private virtual visitation in the agreement

- Factor in travel time/time zone changes

Tip!

The "Home Base" Rule - Design the child's primary residence as "home" for school purposes, and keep duplicate school supplies at your place. Mirror bedtime routines and move favorite stuffed animals between homes.

Modifying Your Schedule

There are three main paths for modifying visitation schedules:

- Informal Agreement: Quickest when both parents cooperate

- Mediation: Neutral third-party helps negotiate

- Court Petition: Last resort (expensive and slow)

Document every requested change and response.

My parenting journal proved invaluable when we needed to adjust for school activities or unexpected life changes.

Key Findings:

- Infants need frequent, shorter visits
- School-age children thrive on predictable patterns
- Teens often require more schedule flexibility
- Always build in make-up days for missed visits

Final Thoughts about How to Tackle Legal Hurdles and Custody

Being a distance dad often means facing legal complexities, but protecting your relationship with your child is worth every challenge.

Through custody arrangements, child support, and visitation schedules, I've learned these systems aren't barriers - they're the guardrails that keep me involved in my child's life.

What began as intimidating legal jargon transformed into empowering knowledge.

Understanding custody types helped me maintain decision-making power across country borders.

Mastering child support calculations ensured I contributed fairly while preserving resources for visits.

Crafting a visitation schedule can be a result of court orders or more about creating predictable moments which your child could anticipate with joy.

The most valuable lesson? Preparation prevents problems.

Keeping meticulous records, understanding modification processes, and using co-parenting apps saved me countless headaches.

These legal structures matter because they protect what matters most - your right to be a dad.

A well-negotiated custody agreement becomes the foundation for many fun times with your child, with the security of knowing you'll always have that next real life or online visit to look forward to.

Legal hurdles aren't about restricting parents - they're about guaranteeing children get what they deserve: the love and involvement of both parents, no matter the distance.

For further reading on the topics in this section, check out the **Sources and References** at the end of this book.

Distance Fathering Challenges

Things to Be Ready For

B eing a long-distance dad brings a different kind of pressure. The usual parenting challenges—discipline, staying involved, building trust—become even tougher when you're not physically there.

And it doesn't stop there.

There's the emotional toll of feeling disconnected, the frustration of not being heard.

And the guilt that creeps in when you miss moments that matter.

You might be dealing with parental alienation. Or struggling to set boundaries from a distance.

Maybe you're trying to stay strong for your child while quietly battling your own mental health.

These aren't small things.

They chip away at your confidence and make you question your role.

This section is here to put those issues on the table.

No sugarcoating.

Just real talk about what you might face.

And how other dads have found ways to cope, push back, and stay present—even when they're far away.

Identifying and Addressing Parental Alienation and Negative Gatekeeping

Parental alienation (P.A.) is a silent and destructive force that many dads experience, especially when divorce and or distance are involved.

It can create an emotional distance between a dad and his child that's hard to overcome.

Often, it's not about physical separation but the emotional toll that gatekeeping and subtle manipulation take on the parent-child bond.

It can be difficult to pinpoint, but being aware of the signs and taking steps to address it can help you preserve the relationship with your child, despite the challenges you might face.

How does Parental Alienation manifest itself?

Parental alienation typically manifests in subtle behaviors that chip away at the relationship between the non-custodial parent and the child.

Common signs include:

- the child becoming increasingly distant

- repeating negative comments about the alienated parent or the grandparents

- showing resistance to spending time with the alienated parent or grandparents

These behaviors can be the result of the other parent's influence, whether intentional or not.

Negative Gatekeeping

Negative gatekeeping, is a manifestation of P.A, when one parent imposes unnecessary restrictions on the other's access to the child.

This could include things like failing to communicate scheduling changes, preventing phone calls, or even using the child as a messenger to relay negativity.

While these actions might not always be overtly malicious, the impact on the relationship can be significant.

How to successfully counter Parental Alienation and Negative Gatekeeping?

If you're facing these challenges, it's important to remain calm and collected. How difficult this may be at times.

Record any incident or behaviors that may indicate alienation or gatekeeping during and between visits .

It can be as simple as keeping track of missed calls, canceled visits, or manipulative remarks.

Clear documentation is essential if legal steps need to be taken later.

Equally important is maintaining a positive and consistent presence in your child's life.

Even if the other parent tries to create obstacles, your love and commitment should remain unwavering.

Be patient, continue to communicate openly, and try to reassure your child of your support and affection.

If things get difficult, consider bringing in a mediator or family therapist to help navigate the situation and improve communication with the other parent.

Inform yourself about Parental Alienation, join Support Groups, such as: Parental Alienation World Wide Support Group or hire a specialized lawyer if necessary.

Key Findings:

- Parental Alienation can be difficult to identify but usually involves a combination of subtle signs such as a child showing disinterest in contact or repeating negative comments about the non-custodial parent.

- Negative Gatekeeping is when one parent restricts or limits the other parent's involvement in their child's life, often through indirect or covert means.

- Early recognition of these behaviors is crucial to preventing further damage to the relationship.

- Keep a detailed record of all incidents that could indicate alienation or gatekeeping.

- Hire professional legal support or counselor

- Consistent and positive communication with your child is essential, as is seeking professional help when needed.

Managing Emotional Well-being and Mental Health

Being a long-distance dad comes with unique challenges, especially when it comes to mental health.

Feeling isolated, disconnected, or even overwhelmed is common among fathers who don't have regular physical proximity to their children.

These feelings can sometimes be intensified by issues like divorce, custody battles, or strained relationships.

But acknowledging and addressing your mental health is a crucial step toward improving both your well-being and your relationship with your child.

Self-isolation

It's easy to feel like you're in this alone, but you're not. There are effective strategies you can implement to manage stress, reduce anxiety, and get back to feeling more like yourself.

Here are 13 steps that can guide you through improving your emotional well-being as a distance dad.

1 - Acknowledge Your Emotions

The first step toward improving your mental health is simply recognizing your emotions. As men, we often feel pressured to keep our feelings to ourselves, but ignoring them only leads to more stress.

Whether it's sadness, frustration, or guilt, allowing yourself to feel these emotions is not a weakness; it's a sign of strength. Being in touch with how you feel helps you process those emotions and move forward.

This is especially important for distance dads, who might feel guilt or frustration about not being physically present for their children.

Accepting these feelings can help you break the cycle of self-blame and create a healthier mindset.

Tip!

If you're dealing with dad guilt, there are specific coping strategies that can help you manage this emotion and find a healthier balance. Consider seeking out resources like the Mental Health Foundation in the UK, which provides insights on emotional health and helps break the stigma around mental well-being.

2 - Seek Professional Help

Counseling is another effective way to work through the emotions you might be dealing with.

Seeing a counselor can provide you with the tools to manage mental health challenges and work through specific issues that are affecting your well-being.

If in-person therapy isn't an option, there are many online counseling services available that focus on men's mental health, offering global accessibility.

Services like BetterHelp offer online counseling, while Psychology Today provides a directory of counselors worldwide, some of whom specialize in men's mental health.

A therapist can help you find coping mechanisms and guide you through your emotional struggles in a way that promotes long-term healing.

Tip!

Therapists can help you navigate complex emotions such as guilt, self-isolation, loneliness, or frustration. They will teach you how to manage those feelings while giving you insight into how to build resilience and improve your overall mental health.

3 - Connect with Support Groups

One of the most effective ways to combat self-isolation, loneliness and improve mental health is to connect with others who are going through similar experiences.

Joining a support group, whether online or in person, can provide a sense of belonging and help you feel less isolated.

Many men's mental health support groups focus on creating a safe space where you can talk openly and exchange advice.

Groups like Movember and the Men's Sheds Association (UK) promote mental health awareness and provide resources for men dealing with emotional struggles.

Engaging with others who understand your situation can offer comfort and build a sense of community that can be especially valuable for distance dads.

Tip!

Check out organizations like Movember, which provide global resources for men and facilitate connections through social platforms, and the Men's Sheds Association, which connects men in the UK through hands-on projects to promote mental health and foster friendships.

4 - Practice Mindfulness and Meditation

Mindfulness and meditation are powerful tools that can help reduce anxiety and stress.

These practices encourage you to focus on the present moment, which can help clear your mind and improve mental clarity.

Studies have shown that mindfulness techniques can be especially helpful for managing emotional well-being, especially for those dealing with depression or high stress.

Apps like Headspace and Calm offer guided meditations and mindfulness exercises that are tailored to stress relief.

Taking just a few minutes each day to meditate can significantly boost your mood and help you manage the pressures of being a distance dad.

Tip!

Try incorporating mindfulness into your daily routine. It's a small change that can have a big impact on your mental health over time.

5 - Establish a Consistent Exercise Routine

Exercise is one of the most effective ways to combat stress and improve mental health.

Physical activity releases endorphins, which are chemicals in your brain that improve your mood and decrease feelings of anxiety and depression.

Regular exercise also helps regulate your sleep patterns, reduces stress levels, and boosts your energy.

Time-mananagement

For many dads, finding time to exercise can be difficult, but even small changes can make a big difference.

Whether it's taking a walk, running, or following along with online workout videos, incorporating movement into your daily life can be a powerful tool for improving your mental well-being.

Nike Training Club and Fitness Blender are great resources for free workout routines that you can do at home, no matter your fitness level.

6 - Build Strong Friendships

Friendships are essential for emotional well-being.

Having close friends you can talk to and rely on creates a support network that's invaluable during difficult times.

Divorced dads and long-distance dads often feel isolated, but reaching out to old friends or joining new groups can strengthen your resilience and provide much-needed emotional support.

Building strong friendships gives you people to lean on during tough times and can provide relief from feelings of loneliness and frustration.

Tip!

Platforms like Meetup offer an easy way to connect with people who share your interests and hobbies, and Movember runs campaigns that encourage men to strengthen their social bonds and build meaningful friendships.

7 - Practice Healthy Communication

Being open about your feelings with trusted friends or family members can relieve a lot of emotional pressure.

Healthy communication isn't just about talking—it's also about listening and being heard.

Learning how to communicate effectively, especially in difficult situations, can help you maintain your mental health and strengthen your relationships.

Many men struggle with expressing their emotions, but practicing open communication with other men can reduce feelings of isolation and allow you to share your thoughts without fear of judgment.

Tip!

The Men's Mental Health Forum in the UK offers valuable resources on communication strategies, while organizations like NIMH USA provide tips for men on dealing with depression and emotional struggles.

Key Findings:

- Acknowledge your emotions as a distance dad.

- Seek professional help, such as therapy, for emotional support.

- Connect with support groups to reduce isolation and gain advice.

- Practice mindfulness to reduce stress and improve mental clarity.

- Engage in regular exercise to boost mood and reduce anxiety.

- Build strong friendships to provide emotional support.

- Prioritize mental well-being to better handle distance fatherhood challenges.

- Strengthen your relationship with your child and improve your overall quality of life.

How to Deal with Dad Guilt?

Dad guilt is a real, powerful feeling that many fathers experience, especially when separated from their children.

It can creep in when you're not around for important events or when work, financial struggles, or even your own expectations weigh on your mind.

The distance, both physical and emotional, can make it feel like you're not doing enough, leading to overwhelming guilt.

What exactly is dad guilt?

It's that feeling of inadequacy and frustration, often when fathers perceive they're not meeting the expectations placed on them.

The guilt is amplified in situations like being absent during milestones, not providing financially as expected, or being unable to spend enough time with your child due to work or custody arrangements.

There are different types of dad guilt, and recognizing them is the first step to managing it:

- Absence Guilt: This is the feeling that you're missing out on important moments, like birthdays or school events, because you're not physically present.

- Financial Guilt: After a divorce, many dads struggle with the idea of not being able to financially support their children in the way they want.

- Work-Life Balance Guilt: Balancing a career with quality time with your child can be overwhelming, leading to guilt about not being fully present.

- Comparison Guilt: When you compare your situation with other fathers, especially those who have more time or resources, it can make you feel like you're falling short.

- Decision-Making Guilt: This type of guilt stems from worrying if your decisions, such as those related to parenting arrangements or custody, were the right ones.

Mum Guilt

Many people wonder how dad guilt compares to mum guilt.

While both types of guilt stem from the pressures of parenting, mum guilt often centers around being the primary caregiver and dealing with societal expectations around motherhood.

Dad guilt, on the other hand, tends to focus on the feeling of not meeting expectations, especially when physical presence and financial stability are at play.

Divorced Dad Syndrome

There's also a concept known as 'Divorced Dad Syndrome', where fathers might overcompensate to make up for the family breakup.

This often leads to indulging their children excessively, which can unintentionally create an imbalance or lack of structure in their parenting approach. While it's important to be present for your kids, it's just as important to provide a stable, consistent environment for them to thrive.

6 Coping Strategies for Dad Guilt:

Managing dad guilt is crucial for building a healthy relationship with your child.

Here are six strategies that can help:

- Focus on Quality Time: Instead of feeling guilty about not being there all the time, focus on making every moment you spend with your child meaningful. Quality matters more than quantity.

- Establish Routine Connections: Regular video calls or scheduled activities can help maintain a sense of presence and connection, even when you're apart.

- Reframe Financial Guilt: It's important to recognize that emotional support and time spent together are just as valuable as financial contributions.

- Set Boundaries: Clear work-life boundaries ensure that when you're with your child, you're fully present. This can significantly ease the guilt about not being there 24/7.

- Practice Self-Compassion: Be kind to yourself. Every parent makes mistakes. Recognizing this can help reduce guilt and self-criticism.

- Seek Support: Connecting with other dads who understand what you're going through or speaking to a professional can provide perspective and reduce feelings of isolation.

By focusing on these strategies, you can effectively manage dad guilt and ensure you're maintaining a strong, meaningful relationship with your child despite the challenges of being a distance dad.

Key Findings:

- Dad guilt is a common experience for many fathers, especially divorced or long-distance dads.

- Recognizing different types of guilt (absence, financial, work-life balance, etc.) is crucial for managing emotions.

- Strategies like focusing on quality time, setting boundaries, and reframing financial guilt help reduce feelings of inadequacy.

- Self-compassion plays a vital role in easing guilt and promoting emotional well-being.

- Seeking support from other fathers or professionals helps reduce isolation and provides perspective.

- Ultimately, these strategies allow fathers to focus on meaningful, quality interactions with their children.

How to Manage Discipline and Authority from afar?

Managing discipline and maintaining authority as a long-distance father can be tough. Without regular presence, it's difficult to enforce rules consistently.

However, you can still be an authority figure by setting a good example and practicing positive parenting.

Positive parenting focuses on rewarding good behavior and encouraging children to repeat it.

The goal is to stimulate positive actions instead of punishing bad ones.

This approach fosters a supportive and nurturing environment even from afar.

When you do get the opportunity to visit your child, these moments should be peaceful and enjoyable rather than emotional rollercoasters.

It's important that visits aren't centered around conflict but are instead moments of bonding, connection, and shared joy.

4 Strategies to manage discipline from a distance:

Be an Example

Children learn a lot from observing their parents.

Even if you can't always enforce discipline directly, you can still model good behavior.

Your child will learn a great deal from the way you respond to challenges and how you interact with others.

When you set a strong example, your child is more likely to follow suit.

Use Positive Reinforcement

Rewarding good behavior is often more effective than punishing bad behavior.

Whenever your child does something positive, praise them for it.

This reinforces the idea that positive actions lead to positive outcomes.

Whether it's verbal praise, a small reward, or a fun activity, showing appreciation for good behavior helps your child understand what's expected.

Tip!

A Goose Board is a great tool for positive parenting. Each time your child shows desired behavior, they move forward on the board. Along the way, small rewards keep it fun — and a big reward waits at the end. It doesn't have to cost much. I picked up this idea from other parents during a Triple P Parenting course, and it worked surprisingly well.

Be Consistent, Even from Afar

Even if you're not physically present, consistency is key.

Ensure that you communicate the same expectations and rules, regardless of the distance.

This creates a stable environment for your child and shows them that discipline is a shared responsibility.

Consistency in your messages will help prevent confusion or mixed signals.

Focus on Emotional Regulation

Teaching your child how to manage their emotions is just as important as disciplining their actions.

Rather than focusing on punishment, emphasize teaching them how to express themselves calmly and effectively.

You can do this through regular communication and by acknowledging their feelings, helping them understand the importance of emotional control.

Key Findings:

- Being a role model is one of the most effective ways to maintain authority from a distance.

- Positive reinforcement encourages good behavior more than punishment.

- Consistent communication of expectations fosters a stable environment.

- Emotional regulation and communication are critical in discipline.

- Visits should be peaceful, enjoyable, and conflict-free to foster positive relationships.

Final Thoughts About Distance Fathering Challenges

Distance fathering presents unique psychological and relational challenges that test even the most dedicated Dad to the limit.

The combined weight of potential parental alienation, emotional strain, guilt, and disciplinary hurdles can feel overwhelming—but these challenges also reveal opportunities for growth and connection.

Research and clinical experience show that successful distance parenting requires three key elements: awareness, strategy, and support.

Recognizing early signs of alienation, maintaining meticulous documentation, and seeking professional guidance from specialists for preserving your father-child bonds across distances.

Mental health professionals emphasize that managing emotional wellbeing isn't self-indulgence—it's a prerequisite for effective parenting.

The American Psychological Association confirms that fathers who prioritize self-care through therapy, support networks, and stress management techniques demonstrate more consistent, positive engagement with their children.

Discipline at a distance presents particular complexities, but family therapists recommend focusing on:

- Consistent communication of expectations

- Positive reinforcement systems

- Collaborative rule-setting with the custodial parent

These approaches maintain authority while adapting to logistical realities.

Ultimately, distance parenting challenges measure not our perfection, but our persistence.

By implementing research-backed strategies and seeking appropriate support, distance fathers can build resilient, meaningful relationships with their children.

For further reading on the topics in this section, check out the **Sources and References** at the end of this book.

Divorced Fathers and Distance Dads Facts 2024

DIVORCED FATHERS BY REGION

TOTAL WORLD : 400M (20%)

35
50
46
60
33
21
150
200
24
37
1.5
3

DISTANCE DADS BY REGION

TOTAL WORLD : 250M (15%)

43%
of 1st time marriages end in divorce (60% 2nd, 73% 3rd)

40%
children are born outside of marriage

31%
higher odds of children with separated parents to drop out of school

25%
of children live without a biological, step, or adoptive father in the home

5.8%
of children live with mother only after divorce. 1.3 % with dads

0.03%
of divorced dads commit suicide. 9 x more than mums.

JOBS WITH HIGHEST DIVORCE RATE

1. Gaming Manager (52.9%)
2. Bartender (52.7%)
3. Flight Attendant (50.5%)
4. Gaming service workers (50.3%)
5. Rolling machine setters (50.1%)

JOBS WITH LOWEST DIVORCE RATE

1. Actuaries (17.0%)
2. Physical scientists (18.9%)
3. Medical scientists (19.6%)
4. Clergy (19.8%)
5. Software Developers (20.3%)

Resources:

Our World in Data

Forbes

Distancedads.com

info@distancedads.com

Follow Us On Facebook!

Today's Landscape of Long-Distance Fathering

Modern Fatherhood: A Global Shift

Modern fatherhood is undergoing a significant transformation. With an increasing workforce mobility, millions of fathers are navigating the challenges of long-distance parenting.

This shift is not just a personal challenge; it's a global trend that affects millions of families and children.

Whether due to divorce, work commitments, or other circumstances, many dads are now engaging with their children from a distance, using technology to stay involved.

Global Impact

Long-distance fatherhood is a reality for many. Approximately 15-20% of fathers are divorced or separated, equating to 300-400 million dads.

Additionally, 10-15% of fathers (200-300 million) live apart from their children due to work obligations such as military service or international careers.

This broadens the scope of long-distance fatherhood, demonstrating its widespread nature.

Shared Experiences

If you're a long-distance dad, you're far from alone.

Understanding the broader context of long-distance fathering has helped me realize that countless other dads face similar challenges.

The emotional strain, the longing for presence, and the commitment to remain active in your child's life are struggles that unite fathers across the globe.

The Divorce Statistics Divide

Divorce rates vary across the globe, often influenced by cultural, social, and legal factors.

Understanding these patterns is crucial to recognizing the diverse challenges faced by long-distance fathers.

- High Divorce Rates: Countries like the Czech Republic and Canada report divorce rates as high as 2.8 per 1,000 people.

- Moderate Rates: The UAE and Australia experience moderate rates around 2.2-2.3 per 1,000.

- Low Rates: Countries such as Vietnam and South Africa report much lower divorce rates, as low as 0.2-0.4 per 1,000.

Additionally, remarriage trends show that only 6% of divorced couples remarry, though those who do have a 72% success rate.

These patterns highlight the diverse nature of divorce, which often leads to long-distance fathering.

Understanding these variations can help us approach long-distance fathering with empathy and awareness.

The Impact on Children

The effects of divorce on children are significant, especially when fathers are absent or distanced.

Some key statistics paint a stark picture:

- Absent Father Figures: Around 25% of children grow up without a father figure.

- Academic Consequences: Children of divorced parents have a 31% higher high school dropout rate.

- Custody Disparity: Only 1.3% of children live exclusively with their fathers post-divorce, compared to 5.8% who live with their mothers.

These numbers underscore the importance of fathers staying emotionally involved in their children's lives, even when physical presence isn't possible.

By being present when it counts, whether in real-life or online, you can help minimize these negative effects and provide a sense of stability and attachment for your kids.

A Silent Crisis: Fathers' Mental Health

Mental health is a critical, often overlooked issue for divorced and distance dads.

The statistics surrounding this are sobering:

- Suicide Rates: Divorced fathers have suicide rates twice as high as married fathers and nine times higher than divorced mothers.

- Systemic Gaps: This disparity reflects the lack of mental health support for separated dads.

As a father, it's essential to prioritize your mental well-being—not just for your own sake but for the benefit of your children as well.

Support systems such as counseling or peer groups can make a world of difference.

I've personally found comfort and support in connecting with other dads who understand the unique pressures of balancing fatherhood and mental health.

Work & Relationships

Certain careers carry a higher divorce risk, often due to stress, irregular hours, or frequent travel.

Here's a breakdown of career-related divorce rates:

*   High-Risk Careers: Gaming managers (52.9%), bartenders (52.7%), and flight attendants (50.5%) face higher divorce rates due to stress and irregular schedules.

*   Low-Risk Careers: Actuaries (17%) and physical scientists (18.9%) have lower rates, likely due to more regular schedules.

Work demands often exacerbate long-distance fathering.

Whether it's frequent travel, long hours, or relocation, balancing work and parenting can be challenging.

Technology has been a game-changer for me, allowing virtual check-ins and shared moments even during busy workdays.

Key Findings:

- Distance Fathering Impact. 25-35% of fathers worldwide are affected by long-distance parenting.

- Custody Inequality Remains. Custody arrangements disproportionately favor mothers.

- Workplace Influences Fatherhood. Career demands often exacerbate family instability.

- Mental Health Challenges Divorced Dads. Divorced and distance fathers face higher mental health risks.

Final Thoughts on Modern Fatherhood

Fatherhood, especially from a distance, can be challenging, but it also holds powerful potential for fathers to redefine their role.

Every child deserves the presence of their father, and despite physical distance, modern technology provides opportunities to be actively involved in their lives.

No matter the barriers—be it divorce, work commitments, or living in different parts of the world—Long-distance fathers can still make a significant impact.

In many ways, long-distance fatherhood pushes us to be more creative, more intentional, and more emotionally available.

Your child has a right to feel loved and supported by you, even when you're not physically there. Whether through video calls, voice messages, or thoughtful gifts, these gestures remind them that you are there for them, no matter the miles in between.

It's not just about being a parent; it's about showing up—emotionally, mentally, and in ways that matter most to your child. The emotional connection you share with your child is not confined to physical proximity, but is strengthened by consistent and meaningful engagement.

Children, even when they grow up in different environments, will always benefit from the involvement of both parents. It's important to be an active, engaged father, whether you're 10 miles away or 10,000 miles apart.

Every effort you make to maintain a meaningful relationship with your child enriches their life and helps provide the stability they need to grow into well-rounded individuals.So, even when the distance feels overwhelming, remember that the bond you have with your child is built on love, commitment, and effort.

Technology has made it easier than ever to bridge that gap—embrace it, and remain the father your child needs. The road may be challenging, but the rewards are immense, both for you and for your children.

For further reading on the topics in this section, check out the **Sources and References** at the end of this book.

The Future of Remote Fathering

Emerging Technologies and Their Potential

When I first became a distance dad, I never imagined I'd be reading bedtime stories in a virtual world or creating fairytales with my child using AI.

But here we are. Technology keeps evolving, and it's giving us new ways to stay present, even from a distance.

Augmented and virtual reality can bring us into shared digital spaces. AI can support us with parenting tips, emotional tools, and creative ideas for bonding.

These tools are starting to reflect what long-distance dads actually need—not just for communication, but for connection.

At the same time, we need to stay alert. Not every app has our kids' best interests at heart. Screen time can overwhelm. Some tools promise connection but deliver distraction. And even the most helpful AI needs a human eye.

Online safety, privacy, and healthy boundaries matter more than ever. This section looks at the opportunities— but also the risks.

It's not about chasing tech for its own sake. It's about using what's out there to show up as dads, in ways that are meaningful, personal, and safe.

AR & VR

Augmented Reality (AR) and Virtual Reality (VR) are starting to offer us the chance to be in the same "space" as our kids—virtually, that is.

We can read a bedtime story in a digital treehouse or play hide and seek in a game where both our avatars run around the same environment.

It gives us an extra dimension to make connections on a deeper level.

It's not science fiction anymore. The hardware is still costly, a bit bulky and not always kid-friendly, but that's changing fast.

AI - source of Parenting Knowledge

AI is another powerful development. As a dad, I sometimes wonder: Am I doing this right? What's normal for my child's age?

AI can now answer many of those questions.

From development checklists to interactive learning games, it can guide us while keeping the fun in parenting.

It's like having a pocket coach who doesn't judge you.

It can also help you find useful resources—whether it's about parenting, communication, or mental health.

Just don't take everything it says at face value.

I always double-check by searching online or asking other dads. AI can be helpful, but it's not perfect.

AI for Co Creation

One of the best use cases for AI I've tried is co-creating content with my child.

We've used simple tools to write custom fairytales together. She picks the characters, I guide the story, and the AI fills in the gaps.

It makes video calls less about talking heads and more about creating something magical together. Even short calls become memorable experiences.

Some dads are already using AI to record short story-book videos. You read, the app animates, and your child can replay it whenever they miss you.

That's the kind of connection tech can create—ongoing, loving, and truly personal.

Internet Safety

As a distance dad, the online safety and security of my child has always been top of mind.

While technology offers amazing ways to stay connected, it also brings new risks—especially when it comes to privacy.

Children, due to their vulnerability, are more likely to become targets for online tracking and malicious behaviors.

Thankfully, several measures have been put in place to protect their digital privacy.

In the EU, for example, the General Data Protection Regulation for Kids (GDPR-K) ensures that companies cannot collect personal data from children under the age of 16 without the explicit consent of a parent or guardian.

Similarly, the Children's Online Privacy Protection Act (COPPA) in the U.S. requires websites to get parental consent before collecting information from children under 13.

Australia and other countries have introduced similar laws to prevent companies from exploiting children's data.

But it's not just about protecting data from corporations. Online safety also involves safeguarding children's personal interactions.

Online Privacy & Security

Many online tools now offer end-to-end encryption, meaning that no one, not even the platform provider, can access the communication between you and your child.

This ensures privacy and safety during virtual calls and chats.

Parents also have more control than ever before. Tools like Google's Family Link allow parents to monitor and control app usage and track the whereabouts of their children.

These tools are essential for remote dads like me, giving us peace of mind about what our kids are doing online.

Even with these tools, we as parents need to actively educate our children.

It's important to talk about the risks of meeting strangers online, recognizing unwanted behaviors, and the dangers of sharing sensitive content (tape their webcam!).

It's part of our role to help them navigate this digital world safely, even as they enjoy its benefits.

Key Findings:

- Emerging tech can help distance dads close the emotional gap.

- AR and VR promise enriched interactive meetings, even when you're far away.

- AI supports you with parenting advice, storytelling, and creating lasting memories.

- Internet privacy laws like GDPR-K, COPPA, and encryption help protect children's data.

- Tools like Google Family Link allow for monitoring and controlling your child's online activity ensuring online security.

- Parents must actively teach children about online risks, stranger danger, and privacy.

Final Thoughts about the Future of Remote Fathering

Technology won't replace your presence—but it can strengthen it.

As a distance dad, I've learned that digital tools are more than just gadgets.

They're bridges. They help us step into our child's world even when we're not physically there.

Whether it's telling stories in a virtual treehouse or creating a fairytale over a video call, these shared experiences aren't about impressing our kids—they're about bonding with them.

AR and VR are becoming more immersive and will enrich our experiences.

AI is becoming more helpful. And together, they're turning long-distance parenting from a struggle into something more hopeful and creative.

Still, no tool replaces the real thing. Tech is only as good
as the intention behind it.

Showing up regularly—even digitally—matters more than
having the latest device.

What excites me most isn't just what's possible, but
what's already happening: dads finding new ways to connect, support, and grow with their children.

These emerging tools offer opportunities to stay involved
in meaningful, emotionally rich ways.

We're not just adapting—we're evolving. And in that evo-
lution, our kids don't lose out.

They gain a dad who shows up—even from miles away.

For further reading on the topics in this section, check
out the **Sources and References** at the end of this
book.

Preparing for Evolving Parenting Dynamics

The Global Shift Toward Shared Parenting

The landscape of fatherhood is changing faster than ever. As joint custody policies evolve worldwide, fathers face both new opportunities and persistent challenges in maintaining meaningful connections with their children.

Understanding these shifts helps us prepare for the future of parenting across distances.

For distance dads, staying informed about these changes isn't just about keeping up—it's about finding ways to thrive despite the obstacles.

Whether it's adapting to new legal frameworks or leveraging technology to bridge gaps, preparation ensures we're ready to meet our children's needs.

Significant shifts in legal reforms

Recent decades have seen significant legal reforms aimed at promoting shared parenting responsibilities:

- Scandinavia leads the way, with Sweden and Denmark making joint legal custody the norm.

- Germany and France emphasize shared decision-making through principles like "Kindeswohl," prioritizing the child's well-being.

- Australia and Canada implemented shared parenting laws in 2006 and 2021, respectively.

Yet reality lags behind policy. In most countries:

- 60-70% of cases still result in sole physical custody.

- Mothers remain primary caregivers in 80% of rulings.

- Practical barriers like work schedules, geography, and lack of support systems limit true equality.

These disparities highlight the gap between legal ideals and everyday realities.

For distance dads, this means navigating not only logistical hurdles but also cultural biases that can undermine efforts to stay involved.

Why the Gap Persists

Three key factors maintain the status quo:

Cultural Biases

• The "Tender Years Doctrine" still influences decisions, presuming young children are better off with mothers.

• Mothers are often viewed as natural caregivers, while fathers must prove their capability.

Systemic Challenges

- Courts prioritize stability over equality, especially in high-conflict cases.

- Defaulting to sole custody avoids perceived complications but may harm children's long-term relationships with both parents.

Practical Barriers

- Job flexibility requirements make shared custody difficult for working parents.

- School district boundaries and housing logistics further complicate arrangements.

- A lack of co-parenting support systems leaves many families without guidance or mediation.

- These challenges underscore why preparation is so crucial. Documenting communication, understanding modification processes, and using tools like co-parenting apps can help mitigate some of these systemic issues.

Building a Better Future

Progress requires action on three fronts:

Legal Reforms

- Stronger enforcement of existing shared custody laws ensures fathers aren't unfairly sidelined.

- Penalties for false allegations protect against manipulative tactics during custody battles.

Cultural Shifts

- Education about fathers' caregiving capabilities challenges outdated stereotypes.

- Media representation of involved dads fosters broader acceptance of diverse parenting roles.

Support Systems

- Workplace flexibility allows parents to balance professional and caregiving responsibilities.

- Co-parenting coordination programs provide structured support for separated families.

By addressing these areas, society can create an environment where all parents—regardless of distance—have equal opportunities to nurture their children.

Key Findings:

- Legal equality in custody doesn't guarantee equal parenting time; practical implementation matters.

- Systemic biases require active correction through advocacy, education, and reform.

- Successful distance parenting demands societal support, including flexible workplaces and accessible resources.

- Children benefit most when both parents remain actively involved, even from afar.

- Understanding these dynamics empowers dads to strengthen their relationships with their child.

Final Thoughts about Evolving Parenting Dynamics

Shared parenting is gaining ground in policy—but practice still lags behind. Distance dads often find themselves caught between evolving laws and outdated mindsets.

Understanding these dynamics isn't just helpful—it's necessary.

Cultural biases, court preferences, and everyday logistics still favor the mother as default caregiver.

That leaves many fathers needing to prove their worth just to stay involved.

The good news? Awareness is a powerful tool. Knowing what to expect helps you prepare and respond.

Whether it's documenting your involvement, understanding legal systems, or building flexible routines, every step strengthens your role.

The future of parenting is changing. And by staying informed, distance dads don't just adapt—we lead the way in building a more balanced and child-centered approach to shared parenting.

For further reading on the topics in this section, check-out the **Sources and References** at the end of this book.

Resources and Support

Finding Reliable Help and Guidance

The miles between me and my child can sometimes feel vast and isolating. I know this feeling is shared by many fathers who live apart from their kids. It's easy to get caught in a cycle of self-reliance, believing I have to shoulder all the challenges on my own.

However, my experience has taught me the immense value of connecting with others who understand.

Accessing Support Networks and Communities

Building a support network isn't about admitting defeat; it's about gaining strength, perspective, and practical advice from those who have walked a similar path.

These connections remind me that I am not alone in this journey and offer a vital lifeline during tough times.

The Power of Online Communities

The internet has revolutionized how we connect. For distance dads, online communities can be a game-changer.

Start your search with targeted keywords on search engines. Use phrases like:

"support group for separated fathers"

"divorced dads or distance dads + [optionally your country/region]"

"long-distance dads support."

Social media platforms are also rich resources.

Explore Facebook for private groups focused on divorced fathers, distance dads, single dads, expat dads, or even groups specific to your geographic area.

Reddit hosts numerous subreddits where individuals share experiences and advice on topics like divorce (r/Divorce) and single parenting.

These online spaces offer the benefit of anonymity, allowing for open and honest sharing without fear of local judgment.

I've found comfort in reading about others' journeys, realizing that many of my feelings and challenges are universal.

Engaging in discussions and sharing my own experiences has often yielded practical tips and a much-needed sense of solidarity.

Exploring Local In-Person Support

While online connections are valuable, don't underestimate the power of in-person support.

Your local community likely has resources waiting to be discovered.

Community centers often host a variety of support groups addressing different needs, including those related to family and separation.

Check their schedules online or visit in person.

Churches and other religious institutions frequently offer divorce recovery programs or general men's support groups.

These can provide a welcoming and supportive environment, regardless of your personal beliefs.

Public libraries sometimes have bulletin boards or online calendars listing local events and support groups.

Your city or county's official website may also have a directory of social services and support organizations, which can include information on support groups.

Attending in-person meetings offers the benefit of face-to-face interaction, which can foster deeper connections and a stronger sense of belonging.

Sharing your experiences in a physical space allows for non-verbal communication and a more immediate feeling of understanding and empathy.

Finding Your Niche: Specialized Groups

Every distance dad's situation is unique.

Seeking out specialized support groups that align with your specific challenges can be particularly beneficial.

If co-parenting with your former partner is a source of ongoing difficulty, explore co-parenting support groups.

These groups often focus on developing effective communication strategies, conflict resolution techniques, and creating a stable and consistent environment for your children across two homes.

For those of us who live a significant distance from our children, long-distance dads' support groups offer tailored advice and connection with others facing similar logistical and emotional hurdles.

They often share creative ideas for staying connected virtually, planning meaningful visits, and coping with the emotional toll of physical separation.

If you are experiencing significant emotional distress, anxiety, or depression related to your situation, prioritizing mental health support groups is crucial.

These groups provide a safe and confidential space to process your feelings, learn coping mechanisms, and connect with others who understand the emotional challenges involved.

Many are facilitated by mental health professionals who can offer valuable guidance and support.

Structured Healing: Divorce Recovery Programs

For a more comprehensive and guided approach to divorce support consider exploring divorce recovery programs.

These programs typically run for a set duration, often several weeks, and follow a structured curriculum designed to help participants navigate the various aspects of divorce recovery.

They often cover topics such as processing grief and loss, developing effective co-parenting strategies, managing financial changes, and fostering personal growth.

Well-known programs like DivorceCare, Rebuilders International, and various local men's divorce recovery groups offer a framework for moving forward in a healthy and constructive way.

These programs often combine the benefits of peer support with expert insights and practical tools.

They can provide a sense of direction and a supportive community as you rebuild your life.

Consider if the structured format and comprehensive approach of a recovery program would be a valuable investment in your healing and future well-being.

Tips for Choosing the Right Support

When you begin your search for support networks, take some time for self-reflection.

Consider your personal preferences and needs.

- Do you feel more comfortable sharing your experiences online or in a face-to-face setting?

- Do you prefer the potential anonymity and wider reach of a large online forum, or do you value the intimacy and local connections of a smaller, in-person group?

- Are you primarily seeking peer-to-peer support based on shared experiences, or would you prefer a group facilitated by a mental health professional, legal expert, or other specialist?

- What are the most pressing challenges you are currently facing in your role as a distance dad?

Answering these questions will help you narrow down your options and identify the types of support networks that are most likely to be beneficial for you.

Don't be discouraged if the first group you try doesn't feel like the right fit.

It's perfectly acceptable and even encouraged to explore different options until you find a space where you feel genuinely understood, respected, and supported on your unique journey as a distance father.

Connecting with support networks is essential for distance fathers.

Explore the power of online communities, the value of local in-person support, and the benefits of specialized groups tailored to your specific needs.

Consider the structured healing offered by divorce recovery programs.

Reflect on your personal preferences and don't hesitate to try different options to find the support that resonates with you.

Remember, building a strong support system is an investment in your well-being and your ability to be the best dad you can be, regardless of the distance.

Final Thoughts about Resources and Support

My journey as a distance dad has taught me that seeking support is not a sign of weakness, but rather an act of self-care and a profound commitment to your child.

The connections I've made with other fathers facing similar circumstances have provided invaluable emotional support.

As well as practical advice, and a sense of community that has helped me navigate challenging times and maintain a strong bond with my child despite the miles.

I wholeheartedly encourage you to actively explore the diverse resources available to you, both online and within your local community.

Remember that you do not have to navigate this path alone.

Building a robust support network will empower you, strengthen your resilience, and ultimately enhance your ability to be the loving and engaged father your child needs.

For further reading on the topics in this section, check out the **Sources and References** at the end of this book.

Epilogue

A s we wrap up this journey together, I hope this book has given you a clear understanding of what it truly means to be a distance dad.

From preparing yourself for the challenges ahead, to recognizing the immense value you bring in your child's development, each section has aimed to equip you with the tools and strategies needed to navigate long-distance fatherhood.

Preparing to be a distance dad is no small feat. It requires understanding the different factors—whether they be emotional, logistical, or legal—that shape your role.

The insights from this book, which cover everything from custody arrangements to maintaining connections with your child, provide a foundational starting point. But let's be clear: this is just the tip of the iceberg.

There is so much more to explore, learn, and apply in your personal situation. Resources and support networks are vast and varied, waiting for you to dive deeper.

Fathers Are Forever

One of the key takeaways is that dads are irreplaceable figures in their children's lives, no matter the distance.

Whether it's providing emotional support, nurturing resilience, or simply being present in small moments, your influence is profound.

The strategies laid out in this book are all about finding creative ways to stay involved, regardless of where you are. It's not about perfection but about being intentional in your efforts.

While it may seem overwhelming at times, the tools and ideas shared—from scheduling visits and legal considerations to staying emotionally connected through technology—are all designed to help you face the realities of distance fathering head-on.

This book should serve as a guide that you can return to whenever you need a reminder or new strategy.

Each chapter, each section, has offered practical insights to help you build and maintain a strong, loving bond with your child.

I truly hope this book has inspired you to embrace the journey of distance fatherhood.

Yes, it's challenging, but it is also an opportunity to create something truly special with your child.

By applying the tips and ideas presented here, you can transform the physical distance into emotional closeness, and make the most of the time you do have.

I encourage you to revisit these strategies, as your relationship evolves.

The world of remote fathering is constantly changing, and there's always something new to learn.

Whether it's emerging technologies, new parenting dynamics, or simply finding new ways to connect, keep exploring and adapting.

Most importantly, remember that the efforts you make, big or small, are the ones that truly count.

This book was just a start. There's much more information out there, much more you can do. But now, you are not alone.

You have a solid foundation, and you have the power to build the kind of relationship with your child that will last a lifetime.

Thank you for trusting me with this part of your journey. I hope you found this book helpful, inspiring, and most of all—practical.

Sources and References

Sources - Introduction

Why Is A Long Distance Father Special? 4 Essential Insights - DistanceDads.com: Explores the unique challenges and opportunities of being a long-distance father. (distancedads.com)

Role Father? 10 reasons why dads are important - DistanceDads.com: Highlights the vital roles fathers play in their children's lives, from emotional support to shaping character. (distancedads.com)

Understanding the Vital Role of Fathers – APA: Discusses the psychological and developmental impact fathers have on their children. (apa.org)

4 Reasons Why Dads Are Essential – Foxconn: Outlines essential ways fathers contribute to child development and well-being. (fox26houston.com)

Fathers Matter – NIH: Peer-reviewed research on the importance of fathers in child development, emphasizing mental health outcomes. (nih.gov)

Dads are Important (OPM) - U.S. government resource (opm.gov)

Judith Wallerstein & Warren Farrell – Beyond Economic Fatherhood: Encourages divorced fathers to stay involved in parenting beyond financial support. (upenn. edu)

Beyond Economic Fatherhood: Encouraging Divorced Fathers to Parent – Discusses how divorced fathers can focus on active parenting beyond just financial support. (upenn.edu)

Father-Daughter Bonds: How Our Dads Shape Our Lives - Explores the significance of the father-daughter relationship and its impact on emotional development. (brparents.com)

Judith Wallerstein, Warren Farrell & Judith Goodman – Beyond Economic Fatherhood - A study by experts on the importance of fathers' emotional and active involvement post-divorce. (upenn.edu)

Sources - How to be a Distance Dad?

How to Be a Distance Dad?

How To Be A Long Distance Father? 25 Proven Tips – DistanceDads.com: Offers actionable advice for fathers managing long-distance relationships with their children. (distancedads.com)

Fathers' Role in Emotional Development – ACP: Explores how fathers influence their children's emotional growth and coping mechanisms. (childpsychotherapy.org.uk)

Fathers are Critical to Child Well-Being (American SPCC) – American SPCC: Discusses the correlation between involved fathers and the overall well-being of children. (americanspcc.org)

Distancedads – Offers articles and advice specifically for long-distance parenting. (distancedads.com)

DistanceParent – Provides resources and advice for parents in long-distance relationships with their children. (distanceparent.org)

What is a Family Care plan - Explains the importance of a family care plan and its role in co-parenting. (sepict. org)

How to Draft a Parenting Plan through Mediation - A guide on creating effective parenting plans through mediation to ease the co-parenting process. (themarkslawfirm.com)

How to Use Credit Cards to Manage Your Budget – Link to resource/article: A financial guide to help divorced dads manage their finances using credit cards. (nerdwallet.com)

Sources - How to keep connected?

How to Keep Connected?

Video-call-parenting-6-proven-tips-to-keep-them-engaged - DistanceDads.com: Offers practical tips for keeping kids engaged during video calls, making long-distance parenting more effective. (distancedads. com)

Sesame Street's Talk - Listen, Connect: Deployments, Homecomings, Changes: Offers advice on how parents can maintain strong emotional bonds with children during significant transitions. (militaryonesource.mil)

Virtual Visitation for Co-Parents - Explores the role of technology in allowing parents to maintain connection with their children remotely, especially in legal contexts. (ourfamilywizard.com)

ClarkLawyer: Video Chat in Parenting Plans: Provides insights on how to legally incorporate video chat into co-parenting plans. (clarklawyer.com)

First Things First: Video Chat Tips - Offers practical tips on how to make the most of video calls for bonding with children. (firstthingsfirst.org)

Communicate by using Instant Messages, Audio or Video Calls (microsoft.com)

Lien Law Firm: Bonding Over Video Chat: Discusses how fathers can bond with their children through virtual visitation. (lienlawfirm.com)

Kinzoo - video chat software for kids: A video chat platform specifically designed for young children to help foster connections during virtual visits. (kinzoo.com)

Caribu (Mattel) - video chat software for kids:: A platform offering shared experiences for kids during video calls, such as reading and drawing together. (caribu.com)

Google Meet - video chat software: A widely accessible video conferencing tool for staying in touch with family members. (meet.google.com)

Microsoft Teams - video chat software: Another reliable option for remote communication with family, often used in educational and professional contexts. (microsoft.com)

Zoom Video Chat Software: A popular platform that enables video calls and meetings, widely used by families for virtual visits. (zoom.com)

Open Broadcast Software - Open Source Video Mix Software: A free, open-source software for customizing video calls with professional-grade features. (obsproject.com)

Voicemeeter Banana - Freeware Audio Mix Software: A tool for improving the audio quality during video calls. (vb-audio.com)

Long Distance Gifts for a Child? How Science Can Help You: Explores research-backed strategies for sending meaningful gifts to children from afar. (distancedads. com)

Child Development Resources

Parents: Toddler Development: A guide to understanding and supporting toddlers' growth. (parents.com)

Early Childhood Development (CDC): Offers insights from the CDC on fostering healthy emotional and physical development in young children. (cdc.gov)

APA: Children Mental Health: Discusses the impact of mental health on children's development and well-being. (apa.org)

How to Master Temper Tantrum Management in 8 Steps: Practical advice on handling challenging toddler behaviors. (https://www.google.com/search?q=verywell-family.com)

Statistics & Data

World Population Review: Provides global statistics on family structures, divorce rates, and child well-being. (worldpopulationreview.com)

OECD Family Database: A comprehensive source for international data on families and parenting. (oecd.org)

U.S. Census Bureau Family Data: U.S.-specific statistics on family structures and child-rearing. (census.gov)

Eurostat Divorce Statistics: European statistics on divorce rates and family dynamics. (europa.eu)

Australian Bureau of Statistics: National statistics in Australia, including data on families and divorces. (abs. gov.au)

Canadian Government Statistics: Provides national data on family dynamics and child welfare in Canada. (stat-can.gc.ca)

Norwegian Directorate for Children: Norwegian governmental data on child welfare and development. (bufdir. no)

Review of Research on the Influence of Parental Involvement on Academic Achievement: A study exploring the positive impact of active parental involvement in a child's education. (wiley.com)

Sources - How to tackle Legal Hurdles and Custody?

Legal Hurdles and Custody

What is Sole Custody? 6 Key Tips if Lost - DistanceDads. com - A blog post about Sole Custody and how a parent can lose it? (distancedads.com)

Divorce Lawyer vs Family Law Attorney - DistanceDads. com: Expert Interview with Dr. Judit Gaál, clarifies the difference between divorce lawyers and family law attorneys. (distancedads.com)

CustodyXChange Co-Parenting Tools: A platform offering tools for co-parents to streamline their custody arrangements. (custodyxchange.com)

Parents.com Legal Guide: A general legal guide for parents dealing with custody and divorce matters. (parents. com)

Grounds for Full Custody (Ashley Andrews): Provides insights into the legal requirements for gaining full custody of children. (ashleyandrewsapc.com)

Child Support: 10 Things Each Dad Should Know - Distancedads.com: Article detailing the ins and outs of child support, specifically for fathers. (distancedads.com)

Mediation Resources

How Divorce Mediation Works - DistanceDads.com: Expert Interview in which Dr. Judit Gaál explains the benefits and process of mediation in divorce, particularly for fathers. (distancedads.com)

What is Mediation? (Commerce.gov): Explains mediation and how it can help resolve family law disputes. (commerce.gov)

JAMS Mediation Defined: Provides an in-depth look at the JAMS mediation process for family law cases. (jamsadr.com)

International Mediation Institute: Offers resources and accreditation for international mediators. (imimediation.org)

Legal Portals

EU Child Custody Search: A legal portal offering resources for fathers involved in custody battles in the EU. (europa.eu)

California Child Custody Help: Provides legal resources and guidance for California-based fathers dealing with custody issues. (courts.ca.gov)

Attorney Differences

Family Law vs Divorce Lawyer (White Legal Group): Explains the differences between family law and divorce lawyers, helping fathers choose the right professional. (whitelegalgroup.com)

Bishop Law Explanation: Outlines the legal perspectives of divorce and custody from Bishop Law. (bishoplawmd. com)

Visitation Rights

Visitation Schedule? 4 Things You Need to Know - DistanceDads.com: A guide to understanding and managing visitation schedules for divorced fathers. (distancedads.com)

Parenting Plan - DistanceDads.com: Explains the importance of creating a thorough parenting plan for divorced fathers. (distancedads.com)

Virtual Visitation Rights: A New Trend in Child Custody Cases: Discusses how virtual visitation is becoming a critical part of custody cases. (austindivorcelawyer.com)

Virtual visitation changes the child custody playing field: Explores how virtual visitation is changing the legal landscape for divorced parents. (rowe-lawfirm.com)

Sources - Distance Fathering Challenges

Parental Alienation & Gatekeeping

Parental Alienation 19 Counter Strategies - DistanceDads.com: Offers strategies for fathers to combat parental alienation. (distancedads.com)

What Is Negative Gatekeeping? 3 Critical Questions 10 Solutions - DistanceDads.com: A guide to understanding and overcoming negative gatekeeping behaviors in co-parenting relationships. (distancedads.com)

Parental Alienation World Wide Support Group (Public Page) - Public page created by Keith R. Marsolek, offering education, posts, and updates around the topic of parental alienation. A hub for those seeking support or wanting to learn more. (facebook.com)

Parental Alienation World Wide Foundation - This is the Foundation's main Facebook page. All following support pages and groups fall under this umbrella. Led by founder Keith R. Marsolek, this subscriber-based service offers global outreach, awareness, and action around parental alienation. Note: This is not a charity — services are offered through subscription. (facebook.com)

Parental Alienation World Wide Support Group (Private Facebook Group) - A private group founded on April 9, 2014, providing a supportive space for those impacted by parental alienation. Run by Keith R. Marsolek, a PA specialist since 1969. Message: "YOU ARE NOT ALONE!" (facebook.com)

Alienated Children World Wide Support Group (ACWWSG) - Free global support group focused on giving a voice to children and parents affected by alienation. Message: "We are here and coming together as a Global Community to speak out and speak up against what is happening to our children." (facebook.com)

Parental Alienation World Wide Support Group Services - This page offers paid services and personalized support for those looking for structured help beyond the free groups. Also founded by Keith R. Marsolek. (facebook. com)

PAWWSG New Brunswick - A local or regional extension of the broader support network, serving the New Brunswick area. Affiliated with the main Foundation and part of the subscriber-based offering. (facebook.com)

Overcoming Parental Alienation (Psychiatric Times): Explores therapeutic approaches for dealing with parental alienation. (psychiatrictimes.com)

10 Tips to Combat Parental Alienation (Weinbergergroup): Practical tips to help fathers deal with and fight against parental alienation. (weinberger-lawgroup.com)

How to Prove Parental Alienation Syndrome (WikiHow): A step-by-step guide on identifying and proving parental alienation in court. (wikihow.com)

Negative Gatekeeping vs. Parental Alienation: Discusses the difference between negative gatekeeping and parental alienation, helping fathers understand both terms. (maciasmayolaw.com)

Mental Health America - Provides valuable resources and support for individuals navigating mental health challenges, including those related to family dynamics and divorce. (mhanational.org)

Mental Health Support

How to Improve men's health - DistanceDads.com: Offers tips for men to improve their physical and mental health after separation. (distancedads.com)

BetterHelp (Online Therapy): A convenient platform offering professional therapy sessions online for mental health support. (betterhelp.com)

Psychology Today's Therapist Directory: Find a licensed therapist or counselor to address mental health issues. (psychologytoday.com)

NAMI Support Groups: National Alliance on Mental Illness offers free, peer-led support groups for individuals facing mental health challenges. (nami.org)

Wellness & Self-Care

How To Balance Your Time and Build a Structured But Flexible Daily Routine - Helps dads build a balanced daily schedule to manage life post-divorce. (medium.com)

Structure your day the Natural Way: A guide to creating a natural, healthy routine to prioritize self-care. (sarah-fischer.life)

Headspace (Meditation): A meditation and mindfulness app to help reduce stress and increase mental clarity. (headspace.com)

Calm (Mindfulness App): Another meditation app designed to improve sleep and manage anxiety. (calm.com)

Nike Training Club (Workouts): Offers free workout routines and fitness guidance for all fitness levels. (nike.com)

Fitness Blender (Home Workouts): A platform with free workout videos suitable for all fitness levels, from beginners to advanced. (fitnessblender.com)

Social Connection

Meetup - A platform to find and join local groups focused on divorce recovery, co-parenting, and mental health. (meetup.com)

Movember - A men's health movement focused on raising awareness and supporting mental health, prostate cancer, and testicular cancer. (movember.com)

Real Men, Real Depression (NIMH): Offers support and resources for men dealing with depression. (nih.gov)

Sleep & Goals

Sleep Foundation Guide: Provides expert advice on improving sleep quality. (sleepfoundation.org)

Sleep Cycle App: A smart alarm clock app that helps track sleep patterns and wake you at the optimal time. (sleepcycle.com)

SMART Goals Framework: A framework for setting clear and achievable goals, perfect for personal growth after a divorce. (mindtools.com)

Addiction & Creativity

Alcoholics Anonymous (AA): A global support group helping individuals recover from alcoholism. (aa.org)

SAMHSA Helpline: Provides resources for people struggling with addiction, offering a helpline for support. (samhsa.gov)

Skillshare (Creative Classes): Offers creative classes for personal development and new skills, a great way to invest in yourself. (skillshare.com)

Intimacy & Relationships

Harvard Health: Benefits of Intimacy: Discusses the psychological and physical health benefits of maintaining intimacy in relationships. (harvard.edu)

APA: Intimacy & Mental Health: Explores the connection between intimacy and mental health. (apa.org)

Dad Guilt

How to Deal With Dad Guilt? 6 Vital Strategies - DistanceDads.com: Offers fathers strategies to overcome guilt when separated from their children. (distancedads. com)

Verywell Mind: Parent Guilt: Provides advice on overcoming guilt parents may feel after a divorce or separation. (verywellmind.com)

Psychology Today: Dad Guilt: Explores common sources of dad guilt and offers solutions to manage these emotions. (psychologytoday.com)

Whole Parent: Divorced Dad Syndrome: A guide for fathers dealing with the emotional challenges of divorce and co-parenting. (wholeparentbook.com)

Sources - Distance Dad Facts

Why 2024 Absent Father Statistics Are Jaw-Dropping - DistanceDads.com: A deep dive into the startling statistics about father absence and its impact. (distancedads. com)

Statista: Divorce Rates in European Countries: Provides statistics and data on divorce rates across Europe. (statista.com)

Australian Bureau of Statistics: Marriages and Divorces: A government resource providing annual data on divorce and marriage statistics in Australia. (abs.gov.au)

Divorce Rates in the World (Divorce.com): Offers insights into global divorce rates and trends. (divorce.com)

Eurostat: Marriage and Divorce Statistics: Provides statistical insights on marriage and divorce in EU countries. (europa.eu)

World Population Review: Divorce Rates by Country: A comprehensive report on divorce rates around the world. (worldpopulationreview.com)

Our World in Data: Marriages and Divorces: A comprehensive report on how the state of marriage is changing around the world. (ourworldindata.org)

Forbes: Divorce Statistics: Insights on divorce trends and what they mean for society. (forbes.com)

Ipsos: Global Views on Fatherhood: A survey showing global views on fatherhood and its changing dynamics. (ipsos.com)

MenCare: State of the World's Fathers 2023: A global report on fatherhood and the impact of father involvement. (mencare.org)

Fatherhood.org: Father Absence Statistics: Offers a detailed look at statistics surrounding father absence in families. (fatherhood.org)

Sources - The Future of Remote Fathering

Why Biased Joint Custody Policy Has 2 Change Now - DistanceDads.com: A discussion about the need for policy reform in joint custody to benefit both parents and children. (distancedads.com)

Parenting Guide to AI: A futuristic look at how AI can help manage parenting challenges, including co-parenting after separation. (internetmatters.org)

What parents can do to protect their children online: The Federal Trade Commission offers guidance on how parents can protect their children from online threats. (betterinternetforkids.eu)

Children's privacy (FTC): Provides tips and regulations about protecting children's privacy online. (ftc.gov)

GDPR-K: A guide to the EU's General Data Protection Regulation for kids and minors. (gdpr-info.eu)

Family Link - A Google app for managing a child's online presence and digital security. (families.google)

Co-Pilot - Microsoft generic AI tool for knowledge, advice, fun and education. (copilot.microsoft.com)

Gemini - Google generic AI tool for knowledge, advice, fun and education. (gemini.google.com)

ChatGPT - OpenAI generic AI tool for knowledge, advice, fun and education. (chatgpt.com)

Sources - Resources and Support

Support Networks and Forums

National At-Home Dad Network – A resource for stay-at-home dads to connect with others, find advice, and access support. (athomedad.org)

Mental Health America (MHA) Group Locator – Primarily U.S.-focused, offering reference for support group structures. (mentalhealthamerica.net)

MeetUp – Platform to find groups focused on divorce recovery, co-parenting, and mental health, with both in-person and virtual options. (meetup.com)

DailyStrength Divorce Support Groups – Offers both online communities and localized meetups for divorce support. (dailystrength.org)

DivorceCare Online – Offers virtual support groups with Christian-based principles, welcoming individuals from all backgrounds. (divorcecare.org)

Dads Divorce Forum – Hosted by Cordell & Cordell law firm, a space for fathers to seek advice on legal issues and parenting dilemmas. (dadsdivorce.com)

Dads with Kids Forum – UK-focused forum offering support on co-parenting, visitation rights, and managing finances post-divorce. (dadswithkids.co.uk)

Reddit's r/Divorce – A large, active community for divorced individuals to discuss experiences and share advice. (reddit.com)

Rebuilders International – Offers support through professional facilitators, focusing on emotional healing and therapeutic methods. (rebuilders.net)

Dads Resources Center – The Dads' Resource Center supports separated and divorced fathers in staying actively involved in their children's lives. It offers advocacy, education, and resources to promote healthy father-child relationships and child well-being. (dadsrc. org)

Dads Resource Center on Facebook (facebook.com)

Faith-Based Support Groups

DivorceCare – Offers a 13-week program with video seminars, group discussions, and workbook activities grounded in Christian principles. (divorcecare.org)

LDS Divorce Support – Provides support for members of the Church of Jesus Christ of Latter-Day Saints experiencing separation and divorce. (churchofjesuschrist.org)

Co-Parenting and Communication Tools

Our Family Wizard – Offers tools to enhance communication between co-parents for smoother coordination. (ourfamilywizard.com)

Local Support for Fathers (Australia and Europe)

Dads in Distress (Australia) – Support service for fathers experiencing separation or divorce, offering groups and online resources. (facebook.com)

The Fathering Project (Australia) – : Offers programs, workshops, and resources to support fathers in their role, particularly through the challenges of separation and parenting. (thefatheringproject.org)

Platform For European Fathers – : Promotes fatherhood, provides resources, and offers support services for fathers across Europe, focusing on improving father-child relationships. (europeanfathers.wordpress.com)

Papilio (Germany) – Offers support groups and resources for fathers navigating divorce and parenting challenges. (papilio.de)

Väteraufbruch (Germany) – : Offers support groups and resources for fathers navigating the challenges of divorce and co-parenting, helping them stay engaged with their children. (vaeteraufbruch.de)

Vader Kennis Centrum (Netherlands) – : A resource center focused on fatherhood, offering information and guidance for fathers facing parenting and relationship challenges. (vaderkenniscentrum.nl)

Stichting Dwaze Vaders (Netherlands) – : Supports fathers, particularly those navigating divorce, by offering advice, advocacy, and emotional support. (dwazevaders.nl)

Nederlands Jeugdinstituut (Netherlands) – : A resource center offering support and information on parenting and co-parenting, helping fathers engage with their children's needs. (nji.nl)

Férfiak Klubja/Men's Club (Hungary) - A Hungarian-based support group for men, including resources for fathers facing challenges in family relationships. (ferfiakklubja.hu)

Apák az Igazságért Kh. Egyesület/Fathers for Justice Association (Hungary) - Offers support for fathers navigating divorce and parenting issues, advocating for fair treatment and fatherhood rights. (apakazigazsagert.org)

Fathers4Justice (UK) - A campaign group in the UK advocating for fathers' rights, offering support and resources for divorced fathers seeking to maintain meaningful relationships with their children. (fathers-4-justice.org)

More About The Author

Danny R. Andreas

Distance Dad, Advocate, and Founder of DistanceDads.com

I'm Danny Andreas, a 55-year-old distance dad to a wonderful daughter. Over the past ten years, I've built a strong, meaningful bond with my child, despite the challenges of distance and legal hurdles.

Through my experiences, I'm here to share the insights and strategies I've developed, so other distance dads can find support and foster deep, lasting relationships with their children, no matter the circumstances.

The journey of being a distance father hasn't been without its difficulties, but the bond I've formed with my daughter has made every effort worthwhile.

My daughter has grown up bilingual, embracing both my native language and culture. The first time she visited my home country, she immediately felt at home—a testament to the connection we've nurtured.

This unique father-daughter relationship has motivated me to discover and create practical strategies to become the best long-distance father I can be. Over the years, fellow distance dads and divorced fathers facing similar challenges have reached out to me for guidance.

As someone who has always enjoyed writing, I decided to start the blog DistanceDads.com to share what I've learned. My aim is to provide insights, advice, and encouragement to dads navigating similar situations.

Why Dads?
Being a distance dad, I understand the distinct challenges fathers face. The experience of distance parenting from a father's perspective differs significantly from that of mothers, and I wanted to create a space specifically tailored to address those nuances.

From a Dad's Perspective
While I'm not a family counselor or lawyer, I bring both academic expertise and hands-on experience to the table.

My natural inclination for research and problem-solving has led me to explore and apply various techniques, resources, and strategies related to long-distance fathering.I've tested different approaches and identified what truly works—though I recognize that each situation is unique and requires a personalized approach.

The heart of all my content is to offer practical advice, strategies, and insights to help you navigate the realities of distance fathering and thrive in your own situation.

Whether you're looking for tips on how to make long-distance fathering work, what defines long-distance parenting, or how to manage fathering time from afar, you'll find valuable resources here.

Stay Connected
For the latest articles, tips, and support, follow us at DistanceDads.com or connect with us on our social media channels: Facebook (distancedads), Instagram (distancedadster), X (distancedadscom), YouTube (@distancedads) and TikTok (@distancedadster). Have questions or want to share your story?

Leave a note and connect with us at info@distancedads.com. We're here to help you build strong, lasting relationships with your children—no matter the distance